RANSOMED
VOICES

ELIZABETH RABY

RED MOUNTAIN PRESS

ISBN 978-0-9855031-2-3
Printed in the United States of America

RED MOUNTAIN PRESS
Santa Fe, New Mexico
www.redmountainpress.us

CONTENTS

Acknowledgments

So many people to thank: my husband, Jim Raby, for his unfailing support and encouragement; my children, Omar and Sara Sobrino; my brother, Andrew S. Nuquist, who told me to write whatever I remembered; my cousin, Jane Laase Becker; my editor, Susan Gardner, who devoted a patient year and countless hours of her time to this project; the Eldorado Writers' Group, who were the first to read many of these chapters; the Wednesday Praise Poets of Santa Fe, who critiqued many of the poems; Christopher Bursk and Patricia Goodrich, who were always ready to offer helpful advice; Thomas Larson, who read several portions of the manuscript; and Reidun Nuquist, Charles Trumbull, and Moriah Williams for their generous gifts of time and technical expertise. Of course, I am responsible for all errors of fact and understanding.

I also wish to thank Michael Sherman, editor of *Vermont History,* for publishing "The Campaign" and Dan Rottenberg, former editor of *Welcomat* in Philadelphia for publishing "The Enduring Shame of the Land of the Free," as well as the staff of the Library and Archives of the Nebraska State Historical Society and of the Friends Historical Library of Swarthmore College for their generous assistance.

Silence is all we dread.
There's Ransom in a Voice—.
— Emily Dickinson

For Jim, who made everything possible

Singing the World

How does someone come to write poetry? What compels a person to write down, in short lines, her experience of the world? Even before speech I sang in my crib mornings and evenings, little scraps of tunes, sounds I heard or made up.

> Mother's voice,
> her face, hands,
> rhythms, clip, clip
> shoes on wood,
> scrape of dishes,
> hiss of steam,
> iron on dampened blouse,
> feel of my soft blanket
> carried always
> against my face

After I acquired language, I couldn't sleep until I had sung the story of my day—everything I had seen, heard, learned, felt, or imagined, or lines from the book of poetry Mother sometimes read to me:

> *"Down cellar," said the cricket,/"Down cellar," said the*
> *cricket...."*
> *"I'm a lean dog, a keen dog, a wild dog and lone...."*

> Touch, moisture,
> pink snowball
> of crabapple blossom,
> red peonies'
> cool scent,
> my first drownings,
> becoming nothing,
> everything,

a handful of soft desire
sitting hidden
among the flowers and beetles
in some vague dream.

I kept busy in my head, dwelt in secret space.

After years of singing to myself, I auditioned for the Junior Choir at the First Congregational Church in Burlington, Vermont. Mrs. S. the director, asked me to sing scales to determine my range. Up and up and up I went, on pitch, reaching the G above high C. Soon Mrs. S. invited me to stay after rehearsal to do breathing exercises and vocalise. Then she recommended I study with Mrs. G., a stately contralto a little past middle age, mostly retired from performance. By ten, I was sure *singing* was my destiny.

I joined every choir and community and school chorus I could find, practiced faithfully, memorized the beginner's repertoire: "Who is Sylvia? What is she, that all our swains commend her?" I loved the beauty of the line, the way the song flowed over and under and with the piano accompaniment that Mrs. G. played with such feeling, and on Sundays as I sang in choir I loved how the organ rolled, sound waves vibrating up through my feet, my body, our blended voices.

At Vassar I continued my lessons and sang in the Vassar College Choir. There was one crucial exception to my joy in singing—as a soloist out there before the public I suffered from paralyzing stage fright.

Nevertheless, settled in Pennsylvania with my first husband, I persisted into my thirties, somewhat managing my insecurity, but never free of it. My performance was always affected by my fear. During my final year in music I continued to take lessons and perform as a paid section leader and soloist. I sang with the Bethlehem Bach Choir, a small chamber group, a quartet, and I prepared some arias from *The Marriage of Figaro* with an opera workshop. Then I developed a sinus infection that led to laryngitis. I fell from song into silence.

In the midst of a divorce, with limited resources, I thought time would cure the breaks, the halts, the stoppages my voice had suddenly become. It did not. Music expressed the emotions that I was too timid to reveal in my actual life. Singing requires there be no obstruction, no hiding.

Despite my performance anxieties, song had been the one continuity in my life, a thread, an organizing principle.

Without a voice, I became more inward and stifled.

A year or so later I wrote my first poem.

In the poem I discovered I could know what I thought, felt, desired, and say it. I wasn't afraid. Poetry gave me a new voice, allowed me to sing the world I see. On the page I was finally free to be myself.

Ballad

Thick pudding warmth slickered
down and down but, hidden
as in cloudy glass or sort of smoke,
a wolfish grin, thin.

That lonely howl could not be mine,
"She's a lumpen sweet.
She's nearly good," I loved to hear,
"a real vanilla peach."

I divided. Wolf who tore,
lest I forgot the lie I lived,
entrails of the dear,
sap engulfed the snarl.

By the time I began to write, the people to whom I hadn't dared reveal myself were dead. If my mother had lived a long life, would I have become a writer? I'm not sure.

While singing solos in public was always problematic, reading poetry has been easy, a pleasure—always in my mind, the memory and model of my mother's expressive voice. There was a long family precedent of speaking in public—my grandfather, a preacher; the regular speechifying of one of my grandmothers, both of my parents, and even, to a certain extent, myself.

I am a rather strained combination of three women—my father's mother, confident and ambitious, a public figure although eager to appear respectably modest in her endeavors; my mother's mother, introspective, sweet, shy, funny, retiring; and my mother who loved her mother but dismissed her example and modeled herself after her mother-in-law.

Ransomed Voices is an exploration of my road to poetry and to a better understanding of myself through the stories of my ancestors.

Except for a moment or a day here, some years there, I've been happy.

I don't recommend my pliability, efforts to defuse and palliate, or hesitancy to contradict or cause trouble. I admire brave people willing to risk everything in their efforts to improve the world, but I have always been a rather uneasy participant in the world of action.

I want to know more about where I come from. My mother and her mother were good storytellers; my father saved the documents. They all are dead. Are the stories real? Can I fill in the gaps? How did all these ancestors influence the woman and the poet I am? I love their language—the vocabulary, the errors and formalities of diction—foreign, almost lost, and yet familiar.

By saving their voices, I save their lives—at least their lives as I understand them—and my own.

SECTION ONE
Relatives Speak

1 ❖ Mother

Edith Wilson Nuquist, 1907–1970
Burlington, Vermont, January 1941

I wanted another child. For a while it seemed it might never happen. When at last I was pregnant, I hoped you would be a girl. Then we would be a complete family—father and mother, son and daughter. The pregnancy felt like it would never end—ten months. The doctor told me not to worry, but I did. I was so uncomfortable.

I was dismayed when I saw you. The doctor said it was the extra time in the womb that had pushed your nose and whole face so off-center. And your head came to a peak at the back as though you were wearing a dunce cap. I was afraid it was a sign. He assured me it wasn't permanent, but I didn't really believe him. You certainly were not the pretty little girl I had imagined. Your long skinny feet and hands were like waving pencils.

After we came home from the hospital, I wrote the folks to tell them about you. I must have been very frank. Mama wrote back:

> As to looks she runs true to form and her name *should* be Elizabeth like mine—how many times I've heard my mother say I was such an ugly duckling and it gave me an inferior feeling—so don't mention it to the child.

Andrew's mother tried to encourage me:

> As for the looks of the baby, that is not to be wondered at considering the evident late arrival and a few days will work wonders in improvement, I have no doubt. It is fine the little one is healthy, and now development and symmetry of form will come rapidly.

I don't know if she believed it or was just trying to make me feel better. I thought the latter.

You and I had been home a few days when suddenly I felt very ill. Your father came home from his office one evening to find me sitting in a kind of stupor on the floor, you beside me and your brother very worried because I wouldn't speak to him.

Burning with fever, I couldn't think. He rushed me back to the hospital. I had developed mastitis. They cut open my breast to let the infection drain. I stayed in the hospital for six weeks. Andrew engaged Lula, a kind and gentle woman, to stay in the apartment to look after you and your brother.

> It took me awhile to love you.
> When I saw you again
> you were already smiling.
> You almost never cried.
> Your sweet nature
> won me over. Calm, so calm,
> you soothed me.
>
> I put you on the sun porch
> in your carriage, wrapped
> in a cocoon of blankets
> against the winter cold.
> You seemed to enjoy
> branches lifting,
> falling with the wind,
> clouds moving across the sky.
>
> You were happy there. Perhaps
> happy in the womb, you
> didn't feel the need to leave it.
> Such a peaceful baby, you
> seemed to be content
> wherever you found yourself.

Your face did gradually become more normal. You kept the dunce cap until you were two. It disappeared when you finally began to speak.

2 ❖ My Journey Begins

Elizabeth Nuquist Sobrino Raby
Burlington, 1943

I crawled after my brother through a hole in the hedge. There in the neighbor's yard was a small circle of water, black and still. Sudden bright movement flashed beneath shiny green leaves that floated on the water's dark surface. My brother gave me the word for this beautiful mystery, "goldfish." It was the summer after my second birthday. This is my earliest memory.

All is blank for a few months until we began our great adventure in September. My brother Andy was seven and had not regained his strength after two rounds of rheumatic fever followed by attacks of Saint Vitus Dance. Pale and drooping, Andy was not supposed to get "worked up." His cheeks squinched again and again. His nose twitched. His lips, held tight together, pressed out and back, out and back, out and back.

The doctor and my parents were convinced that Andy required a winter in a warm climate far from our home in Burlington. It was wartime and there were housing shortages everywhere, but finally a second cousin of my mother living in Tucson offered to find space for us there. She had not yet found a place when my brother, my mother, and I boarded the train. We left my father behind in Burlington to continue teaching at the university. This long journey stimulated my young mind.

The first evening a porter made beds appear like magic up near the ceiling of the car, one for my brother, one for my mother and me to share. We climbed up to the berths on a ladder the porter slid from bed to bed. When we wanted to climb down again, we only had to poke our heads out of our little cocoon and call him to bring it back. I tried it several times. The porter helped me down and walked with me to the water spigot where he filled my pointy paper cup.

Mother had a box of Wheat Thins that we sampled before she put the box in the mesh carrier attached to the wall above our bed. Each time I was awakened during the night by the squeal of brakes or by the sway and bump of the car, I remembered the Wheat Thins and woke Mother for some more. Mother didn't scold me! She gave me another handful. Then I climbed over her to call for the ladder so I could have another paper cup of water. The porter wasn't angry either. It was a wonderful night.

We changed trains in Chicago. Mother told us to hurry, to stay close, to hold on to her coat as she struggled with our suitcases. Crowds of people pushed and shoved us. Voices boomed above our heads. There was noise, noise all around. Everything was moving. We got on stairs that were moving too, falling away beneath our feet. I wanted to get off!

I let go of Mother's coat and began to run, scurrying down past the knees and feet of the big people crowding the stairs around me. Mother's frightened scream stopped me. Unsure, I sat down to wait for the strange moving stairs to stop. Just at the bottom a man in a uniform snatched me up and over the railing. I began to cry.

Mother reached the bottom, put down the suitcases, and saw that Andy was safe on solid ground. She took me out of the man's arms. Her voice sounded strange when she thanked him. She set me down on the ground and swatted my behind.

"Don't ever do that again! Don't you *ever* let go of me on an escalator! You could have gotten caught. You could have been hurt very, very badly."

But there was no time. "Hold on to my coat. Don't let go!" We hurried on. Andy told me I was stupid. I stumbled along.

On the platform we saw far down the track the light of the approaching train. I felt a rumble in my feet that spread through my body. I felt lost in the enormous sound of heavy wheels rolling on the track, the squeal of brakes, the smell of coal smoke, clouds of steam. The vibration sucked me towards the turning wheels. I began to run. I had to touch them.

The first time, in Burlington, Daddy had grabbed my hand and held me until the train stopped. Now Mother dropped everything and snatched me by the arm. I was so glad. I didn't want to go to the train. I was afraid of it, but I couldn't stop myself.

With a last squeal the train came to a chuffing halt. We scrambled down the platform in the midst of a pushing, shoving mob. Mother found our car. A conductor lifted our three suitcases and me up the metal stairs. We found seats.

Then we were at the parsonage in Earlham, Iowa, Grandmother and Granddaddy Wilson's home. There, once again, everything was new to me, including my grandfather and grandmother. They said I had been there once before when I was a baby, but I didn't remember. They told me they were my mother's mother and daddy. I wasn't sure I should believe them. Mother was too old to need a mother and daddy. Granddaddy liked to tease me. Perhaps it was a joke.

Much to my amazement, Granddaddy could stand on his head, walk on his hands, and balance a broom on his chin. His chin pointed up towards his nose like the picture of the witch in my book. He would get down on his hands and knees so that I could climb on his back. I'd hang on while he twisted and turned. He said I was his big spider, and we'd laugh and laugh.

He took us out to help him feed his chickens and look for eggs in the warm straw of their nests. It was dark in the coop, the chickens squawked and fluttered, and the eggs had dirt and feathers stuck to them. The grain and corn we carried to them in a bucket smelled sweet and dusty.

Granddaddy had a big dirt patch he said was a garden. He took Andy and me with him to help harvest potatoes. I thought he was teasing us again, but he dug into the ground with his pitchfork and the dirt came up full of potatoes. Andy and I pulled them loose and tried to sort them for size. Andy didn't think I was doing it right.

Sometimes one had rotted and turned to nasty black slime. It smelled disgusting. Andy and I held our noses and pretended we were sick. Along the tilled rows were leftover tomatoes, bleached and flattened, that didn't smell very good either.

I made friends with a man who came to visit me every day. He taught me my first real joke. "What did the man say when he saw the three holes in the ground?" I didn't know. "Well, well, well!" For the rest of our journey, I repeated the joke to everyone I met.

Many years later Mother told me my friend had been invalided and grossly disfigured by mustard gas in World War I, but I was too pleased to have someone with so much time to talk to me to notice and I was still too young to realize people were supposed to look a certain way.

The weather was good for our visit. My memories are all about being outdoors with the men. Of course I already knew about houses and beds and dishes. I was making my first acquaintance with chickens and wells and what seemed at the time to be endless space for running and for jumping on my grandfather. My mother, I'm sure, was glad to have time to visit with her mother while we were kept busy outside.

Then we moved on, again by train, to Osceola, Nebraska, and the ghostly order and quiet of the house of my father's parents. Although I didn't really understand why, Grandmother Nuquist was away most of the time, in Lincoln. She was chair of the Nebraska State Board of Control that oversaw the state prison, reform school, and other charitable and welfare institutions and only came home on weekends. Granddaddy, ten years her senior, was in ponderous and stately retirement from his little bank, with a housekeeper to take care of his meals and daily requirements. During our visit, the housekeeper was sent home and mother took over the household chores.

Once again my brother and I were left to the company of a grandfather. A huge man of serious mien, overbearing and intimidating to most adults, Granddaddy loved small children. We were soon under the spell of his little rituals. Once a day we were led into his study where, with great ceremony, he would open the bottom right-hand drawer of his roll-top desk. It was filled with unbroken sheets of honey-licorice cough drops. Solemnly he would break off two of them, one for Andy and one for me.

Several times a day I was lifted onto his knees, where his enormous stomach left little room to sit. Granddaddy pulled a gold watch from a pocket in his vest and held it to my ear so I could hear it tick. Every day he walked us to the train station to wait for the arrival and departure of the giant black steam engine and clattering cars. There one huge hand restrained me from my continuing compulsion to run to the turning wheels while he held his watch in the other to time the arrival and departure of the train.

To Granddaddy Nuquist punctuality ranked first among all the virtues. His watch made frequent appearances throughout the day. All his working years, meals were to be on the table at six, twelve, and six. In his retirement, breakfast was served at seven, but he continued to sit at the head of the table, watch in hand, to begin the meal precisely on the hour. If one were even a second late to table, the greeting was a sarcastic "good afternoon."

Nevertheless, my memory of these meals is a sweet silver haze — the tea service lit by shafts of sunlight, the boiled egg in the Blue Willow cup, the bowl of oatmeal, the morning menu as unvarying as the hour at which we ate. Of course, I didn't know how to tell time. I learned to race to the dining room as soon as I was called. Mother, the cook during our visit, must have found mealtimes somewhat nerve-racking.

Soon it was time to continue our trip to Tucson. Granddaddy made sure we packed a big basket of food and put us on the train in Columbus, Nebraska.

3 ❖ Relatives

A small child, I didn't judge.
They were presented to me
as we traveled west, following
the path of generations. I loved them all,
a line-up of relatives who loved me
because they were mine
and I was theirs. My grandparents
were my grandparents, their lives
only what I could see. They had always
been just what they were now—
one a cheerful energy, a buzz and busyness,
one friendly but indistinct,
one a watch, a lap, a deep voice,
one waves of thick white hair, pre-occupied smile.

They were without history because
I was without history. I sponged them up,
watched, sorted, inhaled. My brother, entranced
as well with grandparents, great-aunts
and uncles, cousins twice-removed,
this bounty he had not known.

"How do we get relatives?" he asked Mother.
"We must get a book and have them write in it.
We will save the book a thousand years."

I'm doing my best.

4 ❖ Granddaddy

Andrew Ferdinand Nuquist, 1872–1946,
Osceola, Nebraska, 1904

I knew my Grandfather Nuquist only from our visits in 1943, '44, and '46. I liked him when I was with him. I was pleased to find his letters. I'm glad I like the man revealed there, too — proud and prickly, irritable and civic-minded, outsized in stature and gesture, utterly dependable. He reminds me of my quick-tempered father, although my father was less proud, less likely to take offense at imagined insult. Growing up under the protection of Granddaddy's hard-earned position in the community provided enough security so a man could be less defensive about his dignity.

What am I that I would not have been without Granddaddy Nuquist? He was my father's bulwark, made my father the rock that below my surface of mildness and submission gave me something unassailable I've never lost. I am my grandfather's granddaughter.

A. F. Nuquist

What I knew for sure
was that I didn't want to be
a storekeeper. Mother was upset
when I sold the store after
Father died in 1891.
She was always a difficult woman
to please. She thought I should stay home,
take care of her and the grocery business.
I always knew my obligations
to my mother and to my father's
memory but I was not going to sell

pickled beets and herring
for the rest of my life.
Mother thought constable was a big step
down. When I was elected sheriff
she still couldn't see why I preferred
chasing criminals to having the only Swede
grocery in Stromsburg. I saved my money,
bought land, bought stock, put together
the first telephone company in Polk County,
was the first Swede hired by the Osceola Bank,
made sure Mother had all she needed.

I thought I would never marry,
was pretty well fixed at thirty-one
when I first saw Maud. One look
forever changed my mind —
            her dignity, sweet face
            chestnut hair, cinnamon eyes.
I determined she would be mine.

That morning in 1903 I stopped at the Morning Cup Café to have breakfast with the fellows, as I did most mornings since my days as Polk County sheriff. It was August and although it was early, it was already hot. We finished our meal and were loafing in front of the barbershop, jawing and fooling before we went to business, and, I'd have to say, waiting for the morning train from Lincoln. It was the day the County Teachers Institute was to convene, and we wanted to look over the new crop of teachers.

But when the stage that brought people from the train depot to the hotel pulled up, only one young lady stepped off. She was tall, a head taller than any woman in town, and not a stick like most of the girls, but womanly. She had a pile of wavy chestnut hair. She wore pince-nez, but I could see she had a sweet and lovely face. The conductor handed down her valise. She stood there a moment, looking unsure but straight-backed and dignified in her white starchy dress all fancied up with pleats and ruffles.

The words come right out of my mouth. I couldn't believe I was saying them. Words I had sworn the boys were never going to hear from an old bachelor like me.

"There's the girl I could marry." I crossed over to where she stood, trying to ignore the guffaws and comments from the fellows.

Steady and cool I said to her, "You must be here for the teacher's institute. Let me carry this case on in there for you, Miss."

By this time she was as red as she could be. "Oh, you needn't bother," she said and lowered her eyes, but not before I saw they were a color I'd never seen in eyes before—cinnamon—lighter than her hair or her dark eyebrows.

"No bother 'tall, Miss." I picked up her valise and carried it across the hotel veranda with her beside me, held the door for her, set the case down by the desk and bowed. She said, "Thank you so much." I left.

Outside the fellows began carrying on again. I was kind of public property. If I went with anybody, everybody was interested and tongues did wag. I ignored the comments and went on across the square to open the Osceola Bank where I had recently taken the position of assistant cashier. Governor Mickey hired me so he could attract Swede customers. I spoke Swede before I spoke English, and I knew all the Swedes in the county from my days working in my father's Swede grocery store.

All day the boys made up some reason to stop by to have some more fun at my expense. I wouldn't give them any satisfaction, but I knew I was going to find out who that young lady was. I was going to see her again.

In a small town like Osceola, I didn't even have to ask any questions. People were busy matching the list of attendees that appeared in the paper to the young ladies we saw on the street. Before the institute was finished, I knew her name, Maud Edgerton. I knew she was to be a teacher over to Stromsburg, my hometown, just six miles away, where my mother still lived.

Miss Edgerton was to board with the family of her first cousins, the Elmer Stantons. Her daddy had once been a law partner of Elmer's, but more important to my purposes, Elmer and I had business dealings. We owned some land together, and we had recently started up the Golden Rod Telephone Company.

The county held a reception at the high school for the teachers the final evening of their session. That night Miss Edgerton and I were formally introduced. We had quite a little chance to visit. I brought her punch and cake. Nothing she said or did caused me to change my first impression of her.

I arranged to carry her grip to the late train after the reception, as she was going home to Lincoln until the beginning of the school year. Before Miss Edgerton's train disappeared down the line, I was thinking about all the things Elmer and I needed to get in order, and how it was going to be necessary for me to see him very often in the next few months.

In very short order I was staying over with Mother on Sunday nights, so that I could escort Maud to evening services. That fall it was announced that there was to be a lecture series in Stromsburg during the week. If Maud agreed to accompany me, there would be an opportunity to spend another evening with her, but when I asked her, she said she wouldn't be able to attend with me!

Maud never knew how close I came to not coming back. It seemed to me that she loved me. When she gave me the answer she did, I thought she *felt* love, but she was not going to approve of it in her mind. Her heart and mind had disagreed.

I wanted her to give me an excuse for her actions. I thought she would have a hard time to find one. My questions embarrassed her. When she made up her weak excuses, I decided she wouldn't be troubled by my company all the time—or even part of the time.

The next week was a very long and lonesome one for me. My mind seemed to be very active. First one thing and then another bothered me until I felt restless and dissatisfied. Evenings I tried to read but gave it up. I thought I was tired and lay down, but couldn't keep my eyes closed. I took walks, went up to the bank and cleaned out the stove and the furnace, cut kindling, got coal ready for morning. No matter how I tried to distract myself, it was Maud, Maud, Maud in my mind. I determined to have things out once and for all. Either she'd have me or she wouldn't. If she wouldn't, I'd just get on with my affairs as best I could.

On Sunday I escorted Maud to evening service as usual, and on the way home I said to her:"I love you, Maud, and I want you to be my wife, but before you say anything one way or another, there are some things I want you to think about.

"Sometimes I think I am like a child and have whims, moods, fancies, and times of restlessness as they do. Instead of having a child on your hands, you would have someone harder to manage, a man ten years older than you, one who might say or do things that would cut deeper in your heart than the doings or words of a child.

"To acknowledge a wrong or apologize for anything I have ever done is about the hardest thing for me to do. I do not remember now of ever having said 'Forgive me.'

"Maudie dear, do you realize that you may have a burden on your hands that would be too heavy for you? I tell you so much about myself so that you may know me and determine for yourself, 'Will it pay?' Not for the world would I have you disappointed and have you regret when it was too late."

I told her it was strange what influence and effect a little girl could have on a man even before she knew it. I told her these things no one else had ever heard me utter, but, no matter what her answer, I had confidence my words would be safe with her.

Then Maudie said sweet words I've never forgotten: "I love you with all my heart, dear Andrew. It will be the joy and happiness of my life to make you happy. Papa must give his blessing, but when he knows you, I'm sure he will love you as I do."

I was a happy man that night.

During my years as constable and sheriff, I had seen a good many phases of life. I saw those who at one time supposed they loved each other but drifted apart and now hated each other. Many are the homes I looked into and saw discord and strife. One or other of the parties was just acting a part and was playing with the love of the other as a cat does with a mouse.

Where there is love, everything seems to be as it should be and all are happy. Without it, a home is a hell on earth—discord, jealousy and finally hatred sit on the throne. One might as well be dead as living such a life.

A couple was in the bank the other day and he had bought a new stove for her. While he was at the other end of the counter, she turned to me "Nothing like having a man that has some money, even if there is no love there." I didn't say anything but done some thinking.

Do you wonder that my faith in women wasn't strong? But in Maud I saw something different. I had no fear that she would be like the gold digger in the bank. The first time I saw her I thought she ought to be my wife. She had something that was lacking in other persons. 'Twas a loving disposition, an unselfish influence that came from her heart and encircled me, holding me closer than any chain could. I loved her and wanted that love returned. The world would be very dark without it.

I studied Maud from all sides and I didn't find anything that I didn't like. I compared our temperaments, likes and dislikes, habits, and our views on different matters. I couldn't find why we could not agree and then our love toward one another ought to make us happy.

Overall, I was glad to be what and where I was because now I was in possession of Maud's love. It has been said "that everything done, is to some certain object to fulfill," and it must be so in this case.

5 ❖ Grandmother

Maud Edgerton Nuquist, 1882–1968

Perhaps one of Andrew's attractions for Maud was that he had been elected sheriff on the Populist ticket. There was a long history of activism on Maud's side of the family. Her father, "Old Joe Edgerton," had followed the fortunes of several "radical" parties — first, the Greenback party, then the Farmer's Alliance. He was next a Union Labor candidate for the United States Congress in 1888 and the Populist Party candidate for the Nebraska Supreme Court in 1891. By 1896, discouraged by the nativist, racist elements creeping into the more radical parties as well as by the radicals' waning influence, Great-grandfather became a somewhat disillusioned Democrat.

Even as a girl, Grandmother Maud's passion was for politics, or rather for a government in service to social justice and equal opportunity. For example, she approved of the opinions of James Arthur Edgerton, her brother-in-law, if not, at least once, of his actions:

> The world may be likened to a great ship. There is plenty of room on board for all to ride in comfort. But a few have taken cabins and all the desirable quarters. This forces the many to ride as steerage passengers, while the weak and unfortunate are crowded off into the waves. We are not doing justice by these to simply throw them crumbs. We must get the selfishness out of our hearts, open up the cabins and give all those on board a chance. If we do not — well, some day we may find them battering down the doors. For injustice breeds injustice.
>
> —James Arthur Edgerton, *Glimpses of the Real*, 1903

Maud: Two Days That Changed My Life

L ong before I met Andrew I abandoned the hope of being generally liked; what mattered to me was to be respected. I would never be interested in a man who didn't respect me or himself. I have often been criticized for being too stiff and proud, too careful of my dignity, too cautious in my speech. I really do believe these faults became fixed in my nature on March 22, 1895, the day the *Grand Island Daily Independent* interviewed Papa. Even now, so many, many years later, it's difficult for me to speak about it.

On March 21, 1895, my sister Blanche eloped with our first cousin, James Arthur Edgerton. Papa had encouraged J.A., his nephew, to come out to Nebraska from Ohio to edit and write stories for newly established radical newspapers. Together they had been ardent supporters of the Populist cause, so when Blanche and J.A. ran off together, Papa felt doubly bereft, abandoned, and betrayed. Perhaps that is why my father, on March 22, 1895, agreed to speak to a reporter about the elopement. This is the piece that appeared in our newspaper, the *Grand Island Daily Independent*, on that day. This newspaper article changed me forever.

AGAINST THEIR WISHES

Miss Blanche Edgerton Leaves Home to Marry a Relative against Her Parents' Wishes

Early yesterday morning Miss Blanche Edgerton, daughter of Hon. and Mrs. J.W. Edgerton of this city, left home for Lincoln, to marry James A. Edgerton, a deputy labor commissioner, and a relative of hers. The parents knew of her going and, not having been able to dissuade her from the marriage, used no other means to keep her from the step she was about to take. The young lady was of age and after every argument had been submitted and the young couple still insisted upon immediate marriage, all the parents could do was to submit with silence and regret. Mrs. Edgerton was quite prostrated by the shock and is still in a very weak condition. The young couple obtained a license yesterday at Lincoln to marry, and are by this time, no doubt, united for life.

Mr. and Mrs. Edgerton have every respect for the husband of their daughter and had only the objection of the relationship. Their reasons for remonstrating against the step can best be heard from Mr. Edgerton's own lips. He was interviewed in regard to the matter this morning by an *Independent* reporter and said:

> *This is a very painful subject for me and I would refuse to discuss it only for the fact that I was bitterly opposed to the marriage, and in justice to myself and wife, I wish the reasons for our opposition known, that we may not be judged wrongly.*
>
> *J. A. Edgerton and myself are double cousins, our fathers were brothers, and our mothers first cousins. There was insanity in our mothers' family, J. A.'s mother being insane, and J. A. and my daughter have both inherited highly nervous temperaments from our mother's side of the house. I did not rely on my own judgment in this matter, but consulted a number of prominent physicians and they all agree that there was the greatest danger to be apprehended from such marriage.*
>
> *I laid the matter before J. A. and my daughter and requested them to take time to consider and not be in a hurry, but as J. A. refused to listen or wait, I finally forbad his coming to my house.*
>
> *But he wrote a letter every day, some of which my wife and I read. He was continually imploring my daughter to leave home and marry him. He said he was engaged in a great literary work that would make him famous, and that he would probably be elected president sometime, and that he would set the world afire in the coming revolution, but without her all his literary work would be lost to the world, and if she did not marry him he would commit suicide.*
>
> *This threat overcame all our reasoning and entreaty, and she left home in the morning before we were up and went to Lincoln.*
>
> *We can't blame her so much as she is only 18 and seemed wholly under his control. But for a great moral reformer, as J. A. professes to be, I think he has set a bad example, one that all men who believe in the up-building of the race, mentally, physically and morally, will condemn.*

Miss Blanche Edgerton was quite well and favorably known here, having resided here over a year. She was, as are her parents, a member of Trinity Methodist church and was active in its young people's societies.

I was so humiliated. For weeks and weeks afterward it was torture for me to leave the house. I was angry with Blanche for disobeying

Papa and for spoiling everything, but I felt so sorry for her, too. I thought at the time that her life had been ruined twice in two days, once by the elopement and then from the disgrace of the article. She was only eighteen. Why, why, why did Papa ever share our troubles with that reporter? Ever after I have kept a close watch over my tongue and have sought to keep family business strictly within the family.

And of course, it was all so unnecessary. After Blanche and J.A.'s son was born a year later, Papa and Mama could not bear to remain estranged from their first grandson or from his parents. The families were never as close as they would have been if Blanche had married with Papa's blessing, but the outward rift was mended. Blanche and J.A. had five children. None ever showed a sign of insanity, and all grew up to worldly success and good marriages.

J.A. changed careers about as often as did Papa. He was the editor of the *Rocky Mountain News* for a while, an editorialist for the Hearst papers, wrote books of philosophy and poetry, and in 1928 ran, not for president, but for vice-president on the ticket of the Prohibition Party.

I determined never to marry without Mama and Papa's blessing.

Eventually most people seemed to forget the article in the newspaper. At least they didn't mention it to me. I enjoyed my time at Grand Island High School. My teachers there were extraordinary, especially Edith and Grace Abbott, Grace Bentley Paine and her husband, Bayard Paine. Edith Abbott later became the dean of the School of Social Service Administration at the University of Chicago. Her sister, Grace, was appointed to Franklin Roosevelt's Council on Economic Security. Bayard Paine became a judge on the Nebraska Supreme Court, and he and his wife have been my life-long friends. I graduated in 1900. Stimulated by these fine minds, I wanted and expected to attend the university. Unfortunately Papa suffered another business reverse. He couldn't afford to send me.

I was bitterly disappointed. Instead of the studies for which I yearned, I obtained a position teaching fourth grade in Grand Island. I taught there for two years. It was an honor to be a colleague of teachers I so respected. Then my father sold the house he had built for us on West Third Street, and we moved to Lincoln. I hated to resign, but in those days it didn't seem quite proper for me to live in Grand Island by myself.

Papa was the one who suggested I apply for a position back in Stromsburg, where I could board with Laura and Elmer Stanton, my first cousins. I won the place and in August 1903 attended the two-day teacher training sessions of the Polk County Teacher's Institute in Osceola. This trip was the first I had made on my own without my family watching over me.

When the train reached Osceola I transferred to the little stage that carried passengers from the station to the hotel. As soon as I stepped down from the stage onto the wooden sidewalk, a very large, dark-haired man in a dove-gray suit asked me politely if I were there to attend the institute and could he carry my case. I suppose I should have declined his offer. Normally I would have, but he seemed so mature and serious, not the silly or impertinent sort I had been warned against.

I felt confidence in him immediately and was glad for his assistance. He lifted my heavy bag as though it weighed nothing and guided me to the hotel desk. It felt fine to be walking beside him. He was almost as tall as my father. He left me and my case in the lobby without asking my name or being in any way forward or improper, a most handsome and gallant stranger. I permitted myself to hope I might see him again.

The institute ended with an evening reception at the high school, and there was my dark stranger, tall and distinguished, the ends of his long mustache waxed and curled. He had a red carnation tucked into his lapel. We were introduced in the receiving line. He was Andrew Nuquist of the Osceola Bank. Later he brought me punch and cake, and we discovered that we had acquaintances in common—my cousin Elmer Stanton was Mr. Nuquist's business partner in some matters. Mr. Nuquist's mother lived in Stromsburg, he told me. He visited her at least once a week. When he offered to see me to the train, I was so glad.

The Friday I arrived in Stromsburg to take up my post, Laura told me that Elmer was out in the country with a friend, Andrew Nuquist, looking over some land they thought to purchase. I hoped Mr. Nuquist would come home with Elmer, but I hoped in vain. Elmer returned alone. Mr. Nuquist, I learned, was expected again on Sunday.

There seemed to be several extra days in that week, but at last Sunday came, and early in the afternoon, so did Mr. Nuquist. As we were still at dinner, he waited in the parlor reading a little book I had brought from home. I wondered then if he had any intimation that I already cared for him.

Before he and Elmer departed to continue their search for land, we all gathered in the parlor. In the course of the conversation, it seemed to me that Mr. Nuquist's eyes were often looking in my direction. Catching them once or twice, I could feel a blush overspread my face. I was embarrassed by my failure of self-possession.

I didn't press an invitation for him to come back again, because I had determined before I arrived in Stromsburg that I wouldn't let him see my feelings. Never having cared for boys, I had done nothing to encourage their attentions. My folks used to scold me for being so icy and cold. Mr. Nuquist was not a boy but a man, and I found myself unsure as to how to proceed. I was afraid parading my feelings for him might cheapen me in his opinion. Nevertheless I waited anxiously every Sunday until he did arrive—to see Elmer, of course.

And then one Sunday, he didn't ride the afternoon freight back to Osceola. He told me he had decided to remain at his mother's until Monday morning. Would I attend evening service with him?

After that Sunday, evenings were long, very long in coming. My heart would beat until I nearly fainted when at last I heard his footsteps on the walk. I'm afraid it was difficult to keep my mind on the service as well as duty required. Afterwards we walked about, my hand on his arm. I never strolled with anyone after church until I strolled with Andrew.

I shall always like dark red carnations. He wore so many that fall. I kept the ones he gave me as long as they would last, with one exception. One night he asked me to attend the lecture course with him. I felt I had to turn him down. I was so nervous I picked the carnation he had given me all to pieces. The next morning when I walked to school, there were the ragged petals, red as blood, on the path to remind me that I had hurt him more than I had hurt the flower.

I was dissatisfied with myself that night but also a little vexed with Andrew. He had insisted so hard on knowing why I said no. It was awkward and uncomfortable to answer him. He told me that night not to worry, he didn't have any feelings to hurt. I knew that wasn't true. I knew I had hurt him very much. What I really wanted to do was to put my hands on his cheeks and draw his head to my shoulder and hold him, but I didn't wish to be seen by the public as having a commitment before there *was* a formal commitment between Andrew and myself. I certainly couldn't tell Andrew that he should ask me to marry him before he could accompany me to the lectures.

It was important to me that our actions be proper. I wanted never to be the subject of gossip as Blanche had been because of my incorrect or unseemly behavior.

6 ❖ TUCSON

1943–1944

Of course in 1943 Maud and Andrew's romance, the whole history of their lives, was only an atmosphere, a whisper of long-established habit, a feeling of substance and security that I wasn't eager to leave. I'm sure Mother felt some reluctance of her own. She had left Burlington upon receiving a positive although somewhat vague promise that her distant cousins in Tucson would find a place for us to stay.

Upon our arrival in Tucson, Mother was surprised to learn the place was a bedroom in her cousins' house. She had never met the Foremans until Mr. Foreman greeted us at the train. We arrived on October 28, 1943, and remained until February 15, 1944.

Mother's first letter from Tucson to my father was dated October 29, 1943, while the details were fresh.

Dear Andrew,

Your darling children are in bed and singing songs and visiting away as cute as can be—on their way to sleep. We have twin beds and I will sleep with Elizabeth, or so I plan. The children will bother each other some but seem fine. They were really wonderful on the trip and Andy actually enjoyed it. He was eyes and ears all the way and couldn't wait to reach the desert....

Our train was on time at Columbus. We discovered that we had but one berth, even tho I'd had two ordered for four weeks....

I put the youngsters to bed and then tried to crawl in. My head had to go back under the shelf and I was pretty cramped but got some sleep. In the morning we breakfasted upon pheasant breast and delicious oranges out of our food basket.

As we approached Denver we could see the Rockies and Andy was so thrilled. The Denver station was a madhouse, with standing room almost at a premium. Soldiers, sailors, WAACs, and poor fools like us.

We stood in line for about an hour *hoping* to get a seat on the Zephyr. When the gates were finally opened, people began to fight for seats. We took the wrong direction, but finally got into a boiling car and got one seat. We, along with all the rest, suffered for an hour or so until motion cooled the car....

I have enjoyed the people on the trip for everyone has been kind and good-natured and they take it all philosophically.... A navy man across from us was seeing his wife and baby for the first time in 14 months, and they were all going to El Paso where his brother had a blood clot on his brain from a parachute jump.

At Dalhart we had to go by taxi to another depot. There must have been 150 people making that change. My 10:50 (a.m.) train had gone but they told me to pile on the next one. Otherwise I'd wait until 10:20 the next night. The noon train had been taken off. There must have been twenty cars on this train, and two engines, part of the time four. The whole thing was jammed full with people sleeping and sitting in passageways and in the dressing rooms. One of the above mentioned aviators gave us his seat in one of the more decent of the cars. Have no idea where he spent the night.

I had far too much luggage as usual. There simply isn't room for three persons, coats, suitcases, etc. in one seat. I held Elizabeth all night and Andy curled up as best he could in what was left. They slept some, in fact more than seems possible. My "setter" got pretty tired for I couldn't move, but I did sleep some. It is an impossible situation with that many people in so small a place as trains afford. The trainmen were all courteous and kind but it was too much for them. A man went through sweeping every hour or so and even so couldn't keep up with the rubbish. Toilets clogged, wash basins stopped up, etc., etc. We went back five cars to the diner, but there was a line waiting that filled 1 whole car so we gave up. One dining car couldn't possibly feed that many people.... The train was about half soldiers....

At El Paso we passed a huge army camp and saw Negroes training pack mules. There must be hundreds of mules there. Through New Mexico and Arizona the train did considerable winding. At one time Andy could see both the front and back of the train. Andy kept watching for the desert and wanted it to be real desert and up to exact specifications. He finally saw plenty.

As we approached Tucson we were ordered to pull all curtains and they were kept down until we got off the train. That was almost too much for Andy.

At the station in Tucson there was another jam. As I was vainly trying to sight a taxi Mr. Foreman came up and spoke to me. I had sent them a telegram saying what train I was on.

He brought me out, [Mrs. Foreman] gave us milk and sandwiches, and we hit the beds and went to sleep until Elizabeth started singing in the morning.

I am going to live right here and think I will like it....

The house has five small rooms but fresh and quite attractive. We have good twin beds, a good closet and large chest of drawers. The woodwork is freshly painted, as are the walls. She has given me space in the cupboard and refrigerator. So far we have washed dishes together. She said she was glad I had my own electric iron (I brought one from Osceola). She has a washing machine but I will refrain from using it except on occasion. I can wash by hand. She does the sheets and towels, you see.

The grade school is directly across the street and there is no tuition. I will enter Andy on Monday. It looks crowded to me and to my surprise I notice almost all boys wear overalls. Mrs. Foreman says it is because there is no grass to play on — all gravel or whatever the white stuff is....

Andy spent all day out in the sunshine and seemed happy. We wore no coats and slept last night with open windows and only a sheet for covering. I can't recall ever doing that in Vermont, even in summer time....

I bought several groceries today and believe we will make out. Milk is the only difficult item. The only way to get it is to go to the store right after it comes in. I hope I can keep Andy eating well but imagine my preparations here won't compare with the fat of Osceola and Earlham. I had to stand in line a long time for everything I bought.

I am to pay $10 a week for staying here, and that is to include light, gas, water, etc. as I understand it. That is very fair price and we are lucky. I think I can easily get along on our $100 per. And have some to spare. That is what we wanted to do.

I bought the youngsters a few little things to play with today.

My trunk wasn't in tonight but Mr. Foreman will see about it
tomorrow. I saw it in Denver....

Love to Daddy Andrew. Edith

Despite this optimistic beginning, Mother was soon restless and
unhappy. She tried to keep us occupied and out of the way in tight
quarters we shared with this older couple not pleased by our noisy
intrusion. I must have sensed their disapproval. I remember many
details of our stay in Tucson but not our hosts.

November 7, 1943

Dearest Andrew,

I have the youngsters right under foot for all hours of the day and
have to keep them out of mischief, keep my temper, keep them
decently dressed, etc. etc. Rather trying. It will be nice to turn them
loose as we did before. This is better even so than having Andy in
bed in Vermont. Andy hasn't yet found anyone to play with but so far
hasn't had much pep for extra play.... Think of you and talk of you a
lot. Love, Edith

Mother and I would sit outside while Andy was at school. Mother
sat on the back step but I sat on the ground. It was hard and bare with
long cracks running through it, not like a yard at all. There was one tree
at the side of the yard and long seeds like little propellers were falling
down from it. Mother said she thought it was an ash tree. While she
read, I tried to fill the cracks with the dry seeds. There were so many
cracks that although I worked every day I couldn't fill them up.

November 13, 1943

Dearest Andrew,

Have been rather nervous and worked up over Andy lately and the
difficulty of managing both youngsters in one room. He came home
Tues. noon with a temp. of 101 degrees and then it was 100 the next day.
He didn't go to sleep one night until almost 12—all of which had me
worried. Kept him out of school the rest of the week and about went
crazy doing so. He and Elizabeth have so little to do other than scrap. I
simply could not manage here with him in bed—far from it....

We have done our best for Andy and will have to trust the weather to do the rest. It will surely be a relief when and if he outgrows the kinks. They should both be brown as Indians by spring. I try to protect my face with my summer hat part of the time.

Such sun as we do have here, and such nights—they are almost magic. Drop in some night and we will take a walk. Love, Edith

November 27, 1943
Dearest Andrew,
If you have not already mailed the Xmas things for out here, please do so *immediately* or you will have some disappointed children. I am buying them next to nothing and Andy confidently expects something from you.... When we get home *Old Boy* it is your turn to pay a little attention to your offspring for I will have done my duty.... Love, Edith

Edith

The doctor convinced us this trip
is the right thing to do—Andy's health
still fragile.

Here in Tucson we have a roof and a room,
enough to eat, no bombs falling on us.
Andrew can't be with us, but he is safe
in Burlington.

I know I shouldn't complain
about our inconveniences
when so much of the world
is suffering. When I think
about the soldiers we met
along the way, where they
are going, what they will
have to do, how can I let myself
be unhappy?

Oh, but I am. I've never felt
underfoot before. I've made my own
decisions, been in charge of my life

since I was a child taking care
of my mother. It galls me
to feel in the way, to be forever
shushing the children, to feel
embarrassed and guilty,
judged.

Thursday night,

December 2, 1943

Dearest Andrew,

Tomorrow is your birthday, and as usual I forgot it until this morning
when Elizabeth started jabbering about happy birthday. You won't
receive this now before Monday when wishes for a Happy Birthday
will be out of date....

Yesterday I bought four wooden fruit boxes for 5 cents per and built
the children some toy furniture. A bed, a chair, and table. It was fun and
I did a pretty good job. My intention was to put it away for Xmas but I
can't get myself separated from little bright eyes long enough to do any
surprising. Before I'd finished the doll bed she knew what it was and
had her dolls ready.... Then I tried to buy a toy dust mop (a real one,
but small) at the grocery store — trying to keep it behind me. Needless
to say she marched out of the store carrying it.

I do think that a good present for Andy for Xmas would be one can
of paint and a brush. I will try to get that and then he can paint this
stuff during vacation. He will enjoy it a lot more than if I did it for
him....

I think we were crazy for ever leaving home. Love, Edith

Dec. 15, 1943

Dearest Andrew,

We all are almost overcome with loving thoughts of home when we
start talking. The children and I got started at breakfast and talked
about squirrels, kitties, the prolific gold fish, toys, etc., until it was
almost pathetic. Elizabeth thinks we are coming back to a new house
and seems to understand it all perfectly. She wants to go back and live
by Daddy Andrew. My favorite recreation is thinking of home....

You may have no more letters get thro to you until Xmas cause who knows what will happen to the mail. If not, know that we think and speak of you many times daily and can hardly wait to get home to you.... Merry Xmas, Edith

Dec 20, 1943

Dearest Andrew,

I am so unhappy here I would leave tomorrow if I could—but I can't and will stick it out until March 1st *but no longer*. That will have to suffice and I think it will. I will manage to visit for the month with the parents before coming on.

I exert myself to the utmost to keep out of the way and keep the kids quiet, but you can't tie them down.....

No use worrying you further but *do not ask me to stay beyond March 1st*. Until I hear from you again. Love, Edith

December 24, 1943

Dearest Andrew,

The children are all excited about Xmas and are pretty cute about it. I do hate to have you miss their opening of packages. They have been so good about not opening the five packages which have come and will do so tomorrow morning. They have red Xmas socks to hang up. I have wrapped the things I have and as usual there are several things for them. I got Elizabeth a 35 cent doll which is surprisingly cute and for which I made coveralls. Then I made a pink silk dress and hat for one of her other dolls. Yesterday we washed, ironed and in general fixed up her two dolls and she thought that fun and so did Andy.

One day we took a bus to town and then walked home, taking our time. The buses are so crowded that one should avoid them for many reasons. On our way home we stopped and watched the trains for quite a while and had quite a discussion concerning trains. You will be surprised at how much Elizabeth knows about this trip and everything in general. She is quite a girl and just about keeps up with Andy.

Tell us about your Xmas and we will do likewise. Lots of love, Edith

Dec. 26, 1943

Dearest Andrew,

Your special delivery came Xmas eve at 9 o'clock. I was so glad to get it for the day wasn't right without hearing from you — it had bothered me all day. It had been some time since our ideas had crossed back and forth. I went to bed with a different feeling because of receiving the letter.

In some ways Xmas wasn't too successful here, for after opening their presents the children seemed a little tired and overwhelmed, and didn't know what to do first....

Elizabeth would so like to have a daddy's lap to sit on and occasionally crawls up on Mr. Foreman's lap, but is not at all encouraged to do so.

I shall be so interested to learn what the house prospects are, for we are moving in on you by April 1st — so bestir yourself....

Since I can't see you or share in the Xmas things there isn't much to do but quit writing and go to bed. All I want to write about is the no. of days before we start home — so — Heaps of love and a dozen or so kisses. Edith

January 10, 1944

Dearest Andrew,

You and I really love a home and would thoroughly enjoy it, and we have almost all of our social life in connection with our home.... The children are interested in what we are coming back to and I've even heard Elizabeth say several times that we were going to have a new home. She is worried about how we will get home from the train, and talks about taxis — why I don't know....

If my mother should write and urge me to come I might go to California for Febr. It will depend upon conditions as she finds them there....

Has it ever occurred to you that Mrs. White's wouldn't be half as nice a place to stay if you had two children jumping on her bed, sliding in her bath tub, playing tag in the hall, and sliding on the stairs? Her attitude would be far different and so would yours if you knew she was listening to your every move — inevitably. The place for kids is their own home. Edith

Andy taught me a wonderful game. We'd sit on the edge of the bathtub, our legs dangling inside. Hanging on to the rim with our hands, we'd drop backward. We'd have to be careful not to hit our heads on the floor. We'd pull ourselves up, then drop again and again. We'd laugh louder each time, until Mother came and told us to stop and to be quiet for five minutes for heaven's sake.

January 24, 1944

Dearest Andrew,

Tomorrow is Elizabeth's birthday and she looks all happy and pleased when we mention it. Your father sent $1.00 which we will use for defense stamps for the children's book. Your card and one from the cousins came today. I bought her some nail polish — she has been thrilled to have neighbors put it on for her twice — and some new crayons. Then I bought five little penny tablets, 1 for each of the children and will try to get a nice apple for each. Suppose I'll buy a cake and ice cream. There are no round pans here and I don't have powdered sugar for frosting....

I do not want to move into another rented house, do you? Where nothing is permanent and it's no use to plan for anything.... Love, Edith

January 26, 1944

Dearest Andrew,

Well, I made up my mind and have bought tickets to California for Febr. 15, 6:35 p.m. — tourist Pullman, with two upper berths. The check $25.84. *The Golden State* No. 3

I will spend about two weeks in California and then wait in Nebraska until you are ready for us.... It was either go via California or return to Kansas City and back track to Lincoln so there is little difference. They said I would have a hard time getting connections at Topeka.

How thrilled I was to get your letter today but it didn't decrease any my desire to see you or come home. Heaps of love, Edith

February 3, 1944

Dearest Andrew,

With the accounts I am sending you should be able to figure out about where we stand financially and what you will have left when I return home.... I am anxious to learn what you find available to rent or buy.... It's a shame we have had to squander what you have made this year as we have. But your son is surely enjoying life and looks healthy enuf now.... Lots of love, Edith

February 7, 1944

Dearest Andrew,

I have been intending to tell you that there is a big difference in the kind of flying going on here. For awhile there seemed to be something of a lull but lately many formations of 15 to 18 bombers have been roaring overhead. They are taking their final training and go directly across. *Think*, these are B-24's.

February 16, 1944

Dearest Andrew,

You will be anxious to know that we arrived safely as is the case. Our train was approximately on time and we had our reservations. It was very difficult trying to manage the children in the two separate upper berths, and as usual we had too much junk. The youngsters were too excited to eat before we started and then when we got on proceeded to eat everything I'd brought so I went to bed a bit hungry.... I didn't sleep too well for Elizabeth did some strenuous kicking during the night and the train seemed to do a lot of switching. The children got a pretty good sleep.

[Los Angeles] is one *huge* city. The station was tremendous and I thought it would be impossible to find anyone. However, Uncle Paul and Mother arrived and found us.

It seems so good to see all the family and I know I will have a splendid time. My aunts seem fine to me and it is nice to have

Mother here with us. My Aunt Edith is a very nice looking businesswoman — very trim indeed. Grandmother had a good dinner ready for us which she had cooked herself — even to hot pie — delicious. It seems wonderful to live *decently* again and eat with tablecloths, etc. In fact it seems heavenly to leave Arizona. I didn't realize how I would react to leaving the state….

This is a poor letter but Mother and Grandmother are talking, reading letters, and Aunt Ruth just came excited over a telegram from one of the boy's commanding officers. They lead quite a life here.

Heaps of love, Edith. Wish you could be here.

February 18, 1944

Dearest Andrew,

The children are having a grand time. They play together so happily out in the yard and love to climb in the fig tree. Andy likes to stay at Paul's and Elizabeth at Grandma's. Both are cute, unspoiled, and are well liked by all. My mother acts as tho she can't see too much of Elizabeth. They all think they have excellent minds and vocabularies. Elizabeth says she has two grandmas and one "udder" one. She understands that [my mother] isn't at her real home. In fact there is little she doesn't understand….

Grandmother Jackson is really remarkable. Every day for dinner she has baked a different pie, and without doubt they are the best pies I ever ate or dreamed of. You would never guess that she can barely see for it isn't evident.

This morning Mother, Marjory and I all cleaned different portions of Grandma's house and then the four of us each fixed something different for dinner. We have nice dinners too. Andy doesn't care much for the feminine atmosphere over there tho….

You will enjoy the children so much when you see them and hear what they have to say about the trip.

Again I say I'll be good and willing to leave at the end of two weeks. I dread the trip tho. They say the windows are so dirty on U.P. trains these days you can see little.

Heaps of love, Edith

February 21, 1944

Dearest Andrew,

California has been having unusual weather since our arrival. Mother says it is the first time she has seen rain here. Anyway it has poured for two days and has been very dismal tho not very cold. Hope we have some nice weather while we are here....

Had intended to take Mother and the kids and get away by ourselves for awhile, but it rained so Paul took us to the harbor. We saw San Pedro, Long Beach, and I have no idea what all. We saw huge camouflaged factories and even drove under some of the netting ourselves. We saw many many ships — mostly battleships of various kinds, tho none of them at too close range. We saw ships coming and going in the harbor and huge shipbuilding yards. We saw men loading on a troop transport — swarms of them. We saw camouflaged ships, rusty ships, etc. Then we ate a shrimp dinner in San Pedro where there were many sailors. It was good and I paid for the meal which I certainly needed to do....

As you can tell we are seeing a great deal and Andy is all eyes and ears. He is again missing school but this will in time make up for it.... I am getting no chance to really visit with Mother tho we see each other several times a day. Life is certainly different for her here and she feels a little dizzy.

As to houses--the 3 bathroom house is not for us to buy. I am almost inclined to think we had better rent — for fear Andy may not be able to stand the climate, or something may come up. At least we shouldn't buy something unsuitable or we would be sick after the war when desirable ones are available.

Heaps of love, Dear. Edith

Andy dug a trap to catch Uncle Paul. He wanted to make it like a lion trap with stakes sticking up in the bottom. He dug and dug while I climbed the fig tree. When he finished he was going to cover it with branches so Uncle Paul wouldn't see it and would fall in. When Uncle Paul came out in the yard and asked what he was doing, Andy said, "Oh nothing, just digging a hole." Andy thought it would be a good joke on Uncle Paul.

February 28, Monday

Dearest Andrew,

I will not write again until we reach Osceola. Imagine we will get along since the children are veteran travelers by now and it will be so much better having a section. We do not have to go down to the city station but can get on at a closer one.

Take care of yourself. Heaps of love. Edith

Caliente, Nevada

Thurs. March 2

Dearest Andrew,

Whether I can write is a question. We have a table up with crayons etc. out….

I didn't take our rubbers to California and that was one huge mistake. We stayed out of the rain until time to get on the train. It was simply pouring and we got soaked and our things are a mess…. We rushed out when they announced the train…. We waded water to get on….

Guess we were fortunate that we didn't try to get on in L.A. for we might not have made it. There was a regular mob scene there for crowds were turned away from the coach train even after they had tickets and had checked their baggage. Those trying to get on the Pullman train couldn't buck the mob coming back and just barely got on. Several women said they had never seen anything like it….

We really had a nice time in California. Am so glad I got to see all the relatives. They all seemed like family and as tho I'd known them always. Particularly Grandmother and the aunts. Uncle Paul played with the children a lot and they adored him.

Want to wash Elizabeth and put some things away. We are going again. Love, Edith.

Saturday afternoon, March 4

Dearest Andrew,

We are marooned in a hotel room in Columbus, [Nebraska], and don't know when we will get to Osceola. We woke up Friday morning to find it sleeting and snowing so we couldn't see out of the windows.

It continued throughout the day so that when we reached Nebraska there was a young blizzard on with visibility about zero. The train went slowly, and due to a wreck behind us we were the last train thro for some hours. We got a telegram *after* we left Grand Island telling us to get off there. I had a hunch I should but thought perhaps the family had made some arrangement at Columbus. When we got off the train the agent told us to go to the Thurston Hotel and called a taxi for us — your mother having called him. So here we be.

Today the sun is shining brightly and the snow melting. They are to call us when and if a bus leaves for York — so far no call and it is about three. Your Dad called and said he couldn't get out of his driveway. Imagine they will call again before long.

We have a fairly large room and it has been rather nice just to doze and loaf today. The children spend their time rolling around on the bed, playing in the water etc. Every time we step out they dash for the snow and are crazy to get right in it.

It's a wonder the kids are ok but they seem to be — they haven't eaten right since we went to California. We only pieced on the train. The diner was impossible. I rushed out in Cheyenne and got 1 qt. of coffee and 1 qt. of milk which helped.

Just went down to the desk. The man told me that the bus is to leave at 3:40. Hope they have room for us and our 3 suitcases.

I have but $5–$2 for the room and $3 for the bus fare. Hope it doesn't exceed that. Probably won't.

I can't go anyplace until I get some clothes cleaned.

Will be anxious to hear further from you and will be glad to come on home. Naturally, I don't anticipate the trip. Lots of Love, Edith

Then we were back in the dark house in Osceola. A big dragon embroidered in gold thread hung in waves of blue silk above Grandmother Nuquist's Victorian needlepoint sofa and chairs. In the stillness the scent of Pear's soap and camphor and Granddaddy's strange leathery odor permeated everything. Andy and I wandered around, a little lost in the quiet. We continued our daily walks to the train station, and I sat on Granddaddy's lap to hear his watch, but there seemed to be more empty time in between these adventures.

Our departure for home was delayed when Andy came down with measles and was put in a darkened bedroom. I wasn't allowed to open his door. Mother read him *The Five Little Peppers*. I tried to listen, sitting on the floor of the hallway and pressing my ear against his door, but it wasn't any use.

When Andy was just about recovered, I had my turn with measles. I developed a soaring temperature and aching eyes and was put in another dark bedroom, the blinds drawn tight against the punishing light.

Several times a day, a thick cloud began a slow puffy roll from one corner of the room towards me. I 'd watch its approach with steadily increasing fear. If the cloud reached me, it would kill me.

When the cloud was on the wall beside my bed, I erupted in hysterical shrieks. Mother came, impatiently pounding up the stairs, to reassure me once again that there was no cloud. It did go away while she was in the room. I knew it wouldn't dare come any closer while she was with me, but if ever she should not arrive in time, I would die. I wished she could stay with me longer, but I didn't dare say so.

Timor mortis was indeed upon me. I have never since experienced such terror.

At last my fever subsided and the cloud went away. It must have been a long time since I had eaten much, because I was delighted by a convalescent meal brought to me on a tray, creamed spinach and butterscotch pudding, both new to my culinary experience.

After six weeks my brother and I were sufficiently recovered that we could begin our long-delayed journey home to Burlington. It was near the end of April when, finally, my father met us at the train station. Strangely, I have no memory of the reunion—emotional, I am sure, for my parents. For me, although long desired, it was perhaps a bit awkward and even a little frightening. I had been away from my father, after all, for almost a third of my life.

He took us by taxi to the home he had purchased for us on Cliff Street. It was the house with three bathrooms Mother had insisted was too grand for us.

SECTION TWO

Home

7 ❖ The House

Burlington, 1944

When my father wrote Mother that he had purchased the house on Cliff Street, her first reaction was panic. Ten thousand dollars! How could they afford such an expensive house? How would they make the payments and maintain it on my father's modest salary at the university? Nevertheless, despite Mother's fears, my father persisted.

My mother loved the house instantly. From the day we moved in, it became central to our family. I can't think of Mother apart from her home. She lived in it the rest of her life and, at age sixty-two in 1970, died there as well. The two became so intertwined that even though my father remarried after Mother's death and moved to a house a few miles outside Burlington, as long as he lived he could not bring himself to sell it or rent it to strangers.

The house remained fully furnished, exactly as it had been on the day she died, empty of people except when some member of the family came home to stay for a few days or weeks. It stood there, memory and museum, a shrine my father visited every day to dust and care for and to pick up the mail that he never re-directed to his new home. As you might imagine, his new wife did not accompany him on these pilgrimages.

Mother moved thirteen times as a child. Her father, Walter Wilson, was a Quaker, a superintendent and preacher in the Nebraska Yearly Meeting. The denomination was losing membership and revenue year by year in the Midwest. The family, consisting of Edith, her two younger brothers, and her mother and father, went from one shrinking congregation to the next. In addition to a tiny salary, a parsonage was usually provided. Edith's pride was damaged by what she remembered as a succession of crumbling houses, dark and faded, into which the family dragged its battered furniture. Sometimes the houses had inside toilets, sometimes not.

Despite the family's constant worry about money and their often dismal surroundings, they were expected to entertain an endless procession of guests — parishioners, visiting missionaries, and Quaker lecturers. The material world was supposed to be unimportant to Quakers. Edith was still very young when she decided the congregants were happy to allow her father to be the one to uphold the ideals of plainness and simplicity.

Bright and ambitious, angry with her father and his churches, Edith soon assumed many household responsibilities for her frail mother. She cooked and cleaned and scrubbed and polished, trying, with limited success, to make the houses comfortable and attractive. She worked her way through Penn College in Oskaloosa, Iowa, with the same grim persistence. Valedictorian of her class, she was awarded graduate fellowships to Bryn Mawr and to Western Reserve. She couldn't afford to accept either of them. She didn't have sufficient funds for the train fare. Besides, even then, marriage and home were her real goal. "She didn't want to put herself in a position where marriage would, she thought, be out of the question for years," Edith wrote years later in an autobiographical sketch for one of her clubs in Burlington.

Just before the crash of 1929 and the beginning of the Great Depression, Edith found a job teaching Latin and English in Osceola, Nebraska, for a salary of $1,305.00 a year. As times worsened, it was reduced to $1,000.00, and then cut again to $900.00. Nevertheless, by being careful about every penny she spent, she managed to send money home to her parents each month and to pay down her college loans. For four years she shared a room in a boarding house with a succession of other young teachers.

One day she attended a lecture given by a young man recently returned to his home in Osceola after three years teaching in China and a trip around the world. She was enchanted by his broad perspective and by his white linen suit. It wasn't long until they were courting. After she and my father married in 1933, they moved to Madison, Wisconsin, where my brother was born. The three of them lived in various walk-ups and small apartments while my father earned his m.a. and ph.d. in political science at the university. In 1938 my father obtained a teaching position at the University of Vermont. I was born in Burlington in 1941. The four of us lived in an apartment.

Perhaps this explains why our new home meant so very much to my mother from her first view of it. I don't want to give a false impression. The house was rather plain, a large, sturdy, well-maintained, two-storied white frame house in a respectable neighborhood of similar houses.

When we crossed the wide front porch for the first time and entered the house, we saw Mother's small mahogany desk and the huge Chinese camphorwood chest already in place in the large front hall. As we moved from room to room, we found a fireplace flanked by built-in bookcases in the living room, a bright sunroom, and a corner cupboard in the dining room. There my father had arranged the collected artifacts from those three years at a middle school in T'unghsien, China. Those years and his stories of camel caravans, tiger hunts, armies battling in the school grounds would ring through the house with the sound of adventure, possibility, and a beckoning world like the lid of the rice bowl chiming into its honored place.

China, 1929

My father, apprehensive, climbs
one shaky ladder after another
up sheer rock wall to a shrine,
somewhat reassured
by the stout chain
that hangs beside him.

Should a ladder fail, he hopes
iron links would hold
until rescuers arrive,
but at the summit
he is disconcerted to encounter
chain affixed not to rock
but to fragile final ladder
and the pointed white beard,
ironic grin of the ancient
priest who leans over the abyss
to greet him.

And there is more to the story.
When the frail priest can no longer
fulfill his duties, his obligation—
to leap off the rock. As a child
that horrified me. Now it seems
eminently reasonable—the decision
left to the priest as duty, not sin,
a final freefall, escape into air.

On that day we moved on to the kitchen where Mother, the practical member of the family, admired the green enameled stove that stood on tall spindly legs, the refrigerator sporting a round motor on its top, and the counters of waxed maple. She was delighted with the large pantry and, beyond the pantry, a laundry equipped with a wringer-washer and two black soapstone rinse tubs left behind by the previous owners. There was a big basement and, my father assured her, a full attic.

Upstairs, each of the three bedrooms had its own tiled bathroom. Andy and I considered the bathrooms by far the most distinctive feature of the house. Soon Mother would discover us leading new-found friends on bathroom inspection tours. She was embarrassed by our enthusiasm, but we had spent so many hours of our time in Tucson discussing the possibilities of a new house that we were almost as delighted by the reality of our home as she was.

Finally on this first day, Daddy led us through the kitchen, out the back door, across the cement driveway, and past the double garage to the amazing backyard. There, scent filled the air from bed after bed of spring flowers. A crab apple tree was smothered in pink blooms the size of softballs. A silver sphere of mercury glass and a sundial rested on two ivy-covered columns. In a corner, we discovered a mossy stone bench backed by a hedge of pink roses with petals like crimped paper. In another corner, an enormous weeping birch cast dappled shade over soft ferns.

It was as beautiful as an enchanted garden in a fairy story. *Our* garden. *Our* house.

Father and the house—
twin pillars between which
Mother finally feels secure.
She needs both, loves both.
She hums as she rolls out
pastry in her bright kitchen,
smiles as she waters her plants
in the sunroom. A happy example
for a daughter.

8 ❖ Bears

Burlington, 1944

"The bear went over the mountain, the bear went over the mountain," my father sang while he shaved. Behind him at the door of the bathroom, I stood looking at his thick hairy legs, and then up past his great white undershorts and sleeveless white knit undershirt. I saw the dark hair that rose above his undershirt and climbed the back of his neck. I watched him rub his badger brush across a bar of Ivory soap. He spread a thick coat of white lather across his dark jaw. He swished the brush back and forth in the washbasin and set it back in its cup. "The bear went over the mountain, to see what he could see."

Daddy was as tall as a mountain. Dark hair covered his arms and hands and fingers up to the second joint. He was broad and a little soft around the middle. "The bear went over the mountain."

He was new to me. I knew he was my Daddy and I knew I missed him, but I had been away so long I had forgotten him. "The other side of the mountain was all that he could see." I liked to hear him sing. I liked his big broad middle.

Mother shooed me away. "Andrew, you really should close the door."

Most mornings, Mother, Andy, and I were in the kitchen when Daddy came down to breakfast in his white shirt, the sleeves folded back over the big arms, and wearing his suit pants. We sat down together to the orange juice and eggs and toast Mother had prepared for us.

When it was not holding something, Daddy's left hand was on the table, twitching back and forth, back and forth. Sun from the window flashed on the dark hair as his hand turned. He talked with Mother. Sometimes Daddy's attention was drawn to my brother or me by a dropped fork or careless chewing. He would growl at us, "*Will* you be careful? What's the *matter* with you?"

On summer evenings it was he who whistled us in from wild and sweaty neighborhood games. It was he who drew my bath in the lavender tub. The strong oily green scent of Palmolive filled the bathroom. It was Daddy who washed my back. He rubbed much too hard and I squirmed away from his hard hairy hand, but I'd try not to complain. I didn't want him to call, "Edith." I didn't want Mother to come instead.

9 ❖ Mrs. Hunt Across the Street

Burlington, 1944–1946

A teacher once
before she was lost
to sadness, left alone
in its grasp, but she still loved
language and for a while
was well enough
to share it with a little girl,
story after story,
day after day,
from the precious collection
first read to her son
so many years before.

Each morning she would bend
to the bottom shelf
of her glass-fronted bookcase,
select one from the row
of red leather-bound books,
the crackly paper gilt-edged,
to read to *me*
of a mermaid, dancing princesses,
wolves, houses on legs, a hen,
word magic, magic words
as important to her
as they became to me.
Then depression's chokehold
silenced her again.

A ghost for so many years now,
a beautiful wisp I don't want to lose.

I found Mrs. Hunt our first spring on Cliff Street. She was digging dandelions along the granite curb on her side of the street, while I sat on our curb, poking my bare toe into little pools of black asphalt melting in the sun. She had braids just as I did, but hers were gray and wrapped about her head. As usual, I began the conversation.

"My name's Elizabeth."

"How do you do, Elizabeth? My name's Mrs. Hunt."

"We live across the street."

"Yes, I know."

"We have three bathrooms."

"Oh?"

"My brother and I use the black and white one."

"Mmh."

"My Daddy works up the hill."

"Up the hill?"

"Um-hmn."

"Do you mean at the university?"

"I think so. Daddy bought the house while we were away."

"Away?"

"We had to go to Arizona so my brother wouldn't get sick again."

"Does he get sick?"

"When he's sick, I'm not supposed to bother him."

"No, I would guess not."

"He's supposed to keep very still."

"Is he sick now?"

"No, not now, but he still doesn't like to play with me very much."

"Brothers can be like that."

Mrs. Hunt wiped her screwdriver clean, back and forth across the grass, and stuck it in the pocket of her dark apron. She opened and closed her fingers a few times and then slowly stood up.

"Elizabeth, would you like to come across and have a glass of lemonade with me? I could read you a story."

Of course I would. I followed her up wooden steps to a porch that was like a dim green room, its walls bridal wreath bushes that had grown up to the roof on all three sides.

Mrs. Hunt told me to wait on the big glider while she went inside for a moment. Soon she returned carrying a thick red book with a leather cover. She sat down beside me and carefully opened stiff pages that crackled and gave off a mysterious spicy odor.

An old woman with wild white hair and stockings bagging down around her ankles brought the lemonade. She was introduced to me as "Aunt Grace" before she disappeared back into the house.

Mrs. Hunt read *The Little Red Hen* as she pushed the glider gently back and forth. Bees knocked white petals from the bridal wreath. The petals drifted down to make a carpet for our shadow house. The faded cushions of the glider felt warm and soft against the back of my bare legs and feet.

After that I tried never to miss a day's visit. I would run across the street and knock at Mrs. Hunt's door. She always had time to read to me. Even when it rained, we could hide in our secret house, safe inside the green walls. Once a week, silent Aunt Grace of the slipping down stockings walked the four blocks to McGrath's for groceries, but Mrs. Hunt never left her property. I was the only visitor.

When fall came, we moved inside. The house with the shades always drawn was as dark and gray green as the forests in our stories. Mrs. Hunt sat in her rocking chair to read from her red leather books. I sat on the daybed under the window that faced our porch. As I listened to *The Gingerbread Boy* or *The Little Mermaid*, I arranged and rearranged her collection of satin and velvet pillows, running my hands across their soft surfaces or holding them against my face. Sometimes I could hear Aunt Grace working behind the closed door of the kitchen and, once in a while, she would pass silently through the living room carrying a dust mop on her way upstairs.

When Mrs. Hunt wasn't reading to me, she talked about her son, Junior, a pilot away bombing Germans. She had a picture of him in his uniform next to her chair. I thought Junior was the bravest and most handsome man I had ever seen or heard about. She told me she used to read to Junior, the very same stories she read to me, from the same red books.

Mrs. Hunt began to share Junior's letters when she received them. Sometimes she would smile as she read, and sometimes she would be very quiet awhile after she folded the letter back into its envelope. Now I realize how very lonely she must have been to share her letters with a four-year-old. How frightened. How relieved when a letter fell through the slot in the door addressed in Junior's handwriting. At the time I just put Junior inside our little circle. He was someone special to both of us. I secretly decided I was going to marry Junior when he had won the war and come home.

He did win the war and he did come home. He moved into Mrs. Hunt's house for a semester while he finished a master's degree at the university. Mrs. Hunt seemed very happy to have him there. She continued to read to me, and I continued to think I would probably marry Junior.

I liked him even more now than I had when he was just a photograph and letter. He would always stop to say hello as he rushed in and out of the house. He would ask us what we were reading and come to look over his mother's shoulder at the pictures in the book. Mrs. Hunt never smiled as much as she did when Junior was home.

One day, the very best day of all, Junior brought home a puppy, a German shepherd/collie mix he named Gypsy. Gypsy and Junior and I played on Mrs. Hunt's porch while she watched us from the glider.

But just a few weeks after Gypsy came to live with us, Junior told Mrs. Hunt he was getting married. He and his bride would have to move to the job he had found far away from Burlington. That was why he had brought Gypsy home. Since he couldn't be nearby, Gypsy was to keep his mother company just as I did. I was proud when he told her he was glad she had a little friend. He meant me!

I adapted to the new state of affairs quickly. I wouldn't marry Junior after all, but Mrs. Hunt and I would go on as before, reading together in our green and secret spaces.

Soon after Junior's departure I rang Mrs. Hunt's doorbell. It was Aunt Grace who answered. She told me Mrs. Hunt wasn't feeling well and couldn't see me. That same day, in the middle of the afternoon, I saw Mrs. Hunt walking on her patch of grass wearing bedroom slippers and a housecoat. Her hair was un-braided and un-combed. It looked more like Aunt Grace's hair than Mrs. Hunt's. When I called across the street to her, she didn't answer me. She didn't even look up.

The next day I rang her doorbell. Once more it was Aunt Grace who answered. She told me I had better go home. "Mrs. Hunt can't see you anymore for a while. It will be better if you stay away from the house and off the lawn. It upsets Mrs. Hunt to know you are here."

Confused and hurt, I ran home. I cried and cried. I couldn't believe my Mrs. Hunt didn't want me anymore.

Later the telephone rang. Mother answered and when she hung up, she called me to her. She said it was Aunt Grace who had phoned. She wanted me to know Mrs. Hunt had an illness that made her feel too sad to see anyone, not just me. She couldn't help it.

This had happened before to Mrs. Hunt. That was why Aunt Grace lived with her, and why Mrs. Hunt didn't live with her husband. Mrs. Hunt had been so sad they had gotten a divorce, a word new to me. I hadn't ever thought about a *husband*.

Aunt Grace took care of Mrs. Hunt the way Mother took care of me. Mother and Aunt Grace hoped Mrs. Hunt would feel well enough someday to be my friend again. But it was Aunt Grace who had always seemed strange to me—silent and unsmiling and outside our little circle. I learned that day what I had not yet suspected. It's dangerous to put one's heart in someone else's hand. People don't stay the same. Just because I loved Mrs. Hunt didn't mean she was going to always love me back.

Gypsy, too, was put outside and began to spend her days wandering the neighborhood, her thick coat smelly and unkempt. She would come to sit with me on my porch steps. Despite what Mother had told me, I waited there, looking across the street. I hoped Mrs. Hunt would appear, her hair combed, her apron straight, just the way she used to be.

That fall I started kindergarten. I began to spend more time with people of my own age. The teacher, Miss MacFarland, showed us how to draw a robin and a tree. She poured something she called "war surplus tangerine juice" into paper cups for our snack. It tasted terrible.

I tried to sit next to one particular boy, Christopher, as often as I could. He lived on Cliff Street, too. After school he and I stood together to watch the big boys play marbles. Gypsy would appear from somewhere and plop herself down across our feet. I didn't talk about Mrs. Hunt. Once in a while she would appear in her yard for a few minutes. Sometimes she said hello to me and I said hello back. She never again invited me to cross the street. I became more cautious about talking to strangers, a little more cautious about talking at all.

10 ❖ The Second Coming

Burlington, 1946–1949

As a very young child I closely identified with Jesus. I thought I might be He, resurrected. The gender difference didn't give me pause. At that age I didn't realize being female made me unfit for certain occupations—savior, for example. When I was still in this state of theological confusion, Mother wrote down the words of a song I sang one night when I was six. "O why, O why do people have war? We would be a happy world if we didn't have war. It's my people killing my Lord.... They are smashing what he wanted to be nice."

It seemed to me Jesus, a living presence to me, and I both understood things that others did not. We shared insight and sympathy for people. In my case, at least, that sympathy extended to include insects, plants, and animals. I thought everything had feelings and a voice that were remarkably similar to my own. I knew I didn't want to be stepped on or torn apart or made fun of or yelled at, so I could speak for all creation in opposing such actions. I was sure Jesus and I were in agreement there.

I also understood Jesus' loneliness. I tried to prevent the boys from stomping on the anthills that filled the cracks in the sidewalk or from yelling mean words and throwing stones at the poor old drunken black man who mysteriously staggered up our street from time to time. My efforts only resulted in worse behavior on their part. Now their jeering and mockery were aimed in my direction as well.

Soon I gave up on my attempts to bring people around to Jesus' and my point of view. Instead I tried to look past the evil and search out the good in the people around me.

This strategy came to me from a poem in *Silver Pennies,* my favorite book. The poem "The Vinegar Man" told of a mean hermit who lived in a tumbledown shack. Boys taunted him. After he died, a trunk was discovered among the discarded cans and heaps of clothes. At the bottom of the trunk was a valentine torn in two, but the inscription could still be read, "With dearest love from Ellen to Ned."

I decided everyone had a heart and a hurt. If I looked hard into a person's eyes, she would know I knew. Understanding became my mission. I would be the peacemaker. "Blessed are the peacemakers for they shall be called the children of God." I could bring comfort.

My strategy worked best with old people, worst with boys. Boys seemed to be the exception when it came to having hearts. No matter how sympathetic I tried to be, they still held me down to smear my face with grease or chased me with dog doo on a stick. I tried to avoid boys as much as possible, especially boys in packs.

My greatest challenge, however, was my mother. I loved her. I was desperate for her time and attention, but her always rational tongue could wound me, make me feel guilty. Mother became the one I most urgently needed to understand.

"Mother, Lynne wore her new patent leather shoes to Sunday School this morning. They were so pretty. I wish I could have a pair of pretty black shoes."

"We don't have money for patent leather shoes! You would outgrow them, anyway. You should be glad you have a pair of shoes! They would look better if you bothered to polish them more often. I work very hard keeping your clothes washed and ironed, you know."

"I know."

"I don't like to hear you asking for things. If I think you need something, I'll get it for you. Are you getting spoiled?"

"No, Mother."

"I hope you realize how much we do for you."

"Yes, Mother."

"You are a very fortunate little girl. I hope you realize that. Look at me when I'm talking to you!"

"Yes, Mother."

I think I confused Mother with Almighty God, Ruler of Heaven and Earth, She who did not permit argument. I could not resist her. I could not sway her judgments, especially since they were intended to improve my moral fiber. It was wrong to want party shoes or a dress or a snack. I had so much already, so much more than the children in Europe who had lost everything in the war, so much more than she had when she was a little girl. She would never have asked *her* parents for party shoes. Didn't I feel ashamed for wanting so much? I did.

I told myself I must learn not to want. Mother was correcting me into goodness. Mother didn't mean to be mean. I was learning to turn away from selfish desires, to forgive, to be a better Jesus.

Mother never raised her voice. She was always rational and therefore never wrong.

> Scrape all food particles into the garbage pail
>
> Rinse and stack neatly on the counter,
> glasses at the front, pots and pans to the rear
>
> Fill two pans, one with suds but not much,
> the other clear, the water slightly hotter
> than you can stand
>
> Wash the back of each and every plate
>
> If you should be so careless as to permit dinner
> knives to rest in the pan, water will enter
> their hollow handles and they will be ruined
>
> Dry each dish as though your life
> depends upon it
>
> Remember, I will be watching

I had an easier time understanding my father. He *often* raised his voice. God did not yell; therefore, my father was not God but just a regular man. Unlike Mother, he made mistakes. I was sure I *understood* him. He must *understand* me back, although since he spent his days and evenings at the university, or going to meetings, or giving speeches, my time with him was very limited. My relationship with my father was less intense than my relationship with *God,* my mother.

I was always afraid I would do or say something wrong that would result in my mother's disapproval or, if we were in public, her embarrassment and shame. I tried very hard to be good. People outside the house seemed to think I *was* a good girl, but my mother let me know it was wrong to feel proud about the nice thing someone said about me. I should never forget that I was nothing special.

To my relatively yielding nature, my mother's implacable character was overwhelming. I was unable to oppose it. As an alternative, determined to be as selfless as Jesus, I wandered the neighborhood looking for people who needed my special understanding.

11 ❖ Two Weeks in 1948

A shale cliff above the lake—a compound of spacious
screened-porch summer houses—our cottage the poor

relation, a dim room set on cement blocks, an island
in a pond of garter snakes that created its own weather,

an endless undulation of trillium and ferns,
the roil and boil of coiling waves—a raised path of beaten

grass our bridge across their mass. Four cots, a folding table
and chairs, a camp stove, a kerosene lamp could not

have kept Mother busy, but only once do I remember her
with us on the beach, pale and awkward in a limp wool suit.

What did she do while we played cards on the porches
where the other women smoked, sipped long summer drinks,

gossiped on musty kapok lounges? I see her, in an apron
edged in rickrack, a housedress she had made herself,

sweeping the bare floor. Summer leisure forever foreign
to her nature, never at home in the life she achieved.

12 ❖ Romance

Compulsive rummages
through Mother's dark
mahogany dresser, its
narrow middle drawer
lined in pale wood —
folded handkerchiefs,
patterned linen and Swiss lace.
One of silk chiffon, its lilies
of the valley, purple pansy, tied
with a curling ribbon of blue,
worked in tiny cross-stitch.
Beneath them all, a bottle
of Chanel No. 5, crystal-
stoppered, sent by her sailor-
brother from far *Paree.*
The unused scent, the whisper
of chiffon clinging to my probing
fingers — the beautiful secret
mother I desired.

13 ❖ Beds

I was given my old white crib, brought out of storage with the rest of our furniture, after our return from Tucson and move into the house on Cliff Street. Although the side rails were lowered, I was embarrassed to be in a baby bed at age three. When I stretched out, my head pressed against the slats at one end, my feet at the other.

The crib was put in a corner of my brother's room. Andy wasn't happy to have me there. Every night I sang myself to sleep and very early in the mornings sang myself awake. He ordered me to shut up, but I couldn't. I could neither go to sleep nor wake up without my songs. I sang about my day, everything I had seen and done, or about what I remembered. I sang about our trip to Tucson, about trains and grandparents and cactus. I accompanied my musical stories by a rhythmic rolling from side to side that made the crib creak and groan. I knew my brother wasn't listening but I imagined an audience. I think I was talking to God. I was sure *someone* was listening. Perhaps poetry fills the same need—utterance in the belief someone will hear you.

My parents answered my brother's frequent complaints by reminding him that I had "rolled and sung" since I was a small baby, long before I had any words to put with my music. They had tried everything they could think of to stop me, but no admonition had any effect.

Eventually, they took pity on us both. On my fourth birthday in January of 1945, deliverymen brought a stack of dark wood into the house. They were directed to take it upstairs to the far end of my parents' long bedroom and place it by the window that looked out over the lake a mile away down the hill. Next they brought in a mattress.

"It's a bed," I said. "A real bed! Is it for me?"

"Yes," my father said. "It's your birthday present."

When it was all put together, the bed appeared to be very long with plenty of room for my head and feet. It had four tall posts and my father pointed out the carved pineapple on each. He told me the bed was made of mahogany. It was so high that I first had to haul myself onto the side rail and then hoist myself up the rest of the way. When I got up there I felt like a princess, the princess who slept on the pile of mattresses to shield her from the pea.

My mother showed me shelves made from an orange crate she placed against the wall between my bed and the window. There was room on the shelves for my dolls, their dishes, pots and pans, spoons, rolling pin, strainer, and cookie cutters. There was a little dresser with three drawers, two for doll clothes and one to hold my underwear. I could play here whenever I wanted, as long as I put everything away when I finished. Mother took me to their big closet where she had hung my dresses on the lower rod so I could reach them. I was very satisfied with this new arrangement, and Andy was happy to have his room to himself.

Our third bedroom had been rented out to a Miss C. very soon after we settled into the house. She was a publicist from New York City who was in town to prepare a fund-raising campaign for the Bishop De Goesbriand Hospital. She had black hair pulled into a heavy roll at the base of her neck. She wore dark silk dresses and high heels with holes cut out at the toe, and her teeth made an odd click when she talked.

Miss C. arranged for me to be part of her campaign. One day Mother fixed my hair in tight French braids and dressed me in the red silk dress with the white lace collar sent from Nebraska after my cousin Jane had outgrown it. Miss C. drove me to the hospital in her black coupe. I asked to ride in the rumble seat but she said no.

In the lobby of the hospital, a man with a camera told me to smile at a nun who took my hand. I was a little uncertain about the nun. She was wearing long white robes and a long white shawl over her head. I had never been close to a nun before. I didn't know if I was expected to act some special way to her, to look down at the floor, to kneel or curtsey, but she seemed kind, and I forgot to be nervous. The man took a lot of pictures of us.

Then Miss C. took me into a small room that smelled of medicine. A nurse lifted me onto a leather-covered table and put a white gown over my dress. She wrapped my head and one arm in gauze bandages and put the other in a sling. Miss C. told me to look sad, and the man took more pictures of me.

Miss C. explained they were pretending I had been hurt in an accident. The picture with the nun was supposed to be after the hospital had made me well again. They took the pictures in the wrong order because Miss C. was afraid she would not be able to make my braids as tight as my mother could.

My pictures were going to be put into a little booklet and mailed out to almost everyone in Burlington. Miss C. hoped they would make people feel like sending money to build a new wing on the hospital. I hadn't really been in an accident. I didn't think it was right. To me, the pictures seemed like a lie, but I didn't say anything to Miss C.

Miss C. stayed with us for two-and-a-half years. Very soon after she moved out of our front bedroom and Granddaddy Wilson had retired from his last Quaker meeting, Mother's parents moved into it. I remained in my single bed at the end of the room beyond my mother and father's big bed. I continued to sing at night and in the morning. It didn't bother them because they came to bed long after I was asleep, and they woke early in the morning.

I remained there until April Fools' Day of the year I turned ten. At midnight the alarm on the clock began to ring. The three of us leapt up. Just about the time Andy ran into the room calling "April Fool!" my father turned on the light and located the clock under his bed. My father did not think Andy's joke was at all funny.

"You chucklehead!" he yelled. "What do you think you're doing?" My father's face was red and he was breathing fast. My father was often impatient but not usually this angry. "What's the matter with you?"

Mother said, "Now, Andrew. Now, Andrew," but it didn't calm him the way it usually did. Finally we all settled down, although my father continued to grumble on in the dark for a while. It was years before it occurred to me that the alarm might have interrupted some activity other than sleep.

The next day when I got home from school, Mother and Daddy were on the first floor rearranging the sunroom. Mother told me she and my father thought it was time I had my own place to sleep. My father had purchased a new bed frame for my mattress. Mother set it up with pillows and a throw from India to look like a sofa. The mahogany bed was put up in the attic. They placed two bookcases in the middle of the room to act as dividers. The upright piano was still in my half of the room. Mother's worktable, the typewriter, and her plants were at the end in front of the big glass doors to the living room. I wasn't happy about this change. I had been very content with my corner of their room, but I could see there wasn't any use arguing.

That evening from my new bed, I could hear the murmur of my parents' voices. Just enough light came through the glass doors and over the bookcases to keep me aware I was in a new place. It took me a long time to get to sleep. Then sometime in the night I woke up, badly needing to pee. But now the bathroom was far away across cold linoleum and around the bookcases, past the dark living room and front hall, and up the staircase. I lay there jiggling my legs until it was barely light. Finally I made an uncomfortable dash to the bathroom. I never did get used to that run. None of us thought of a night-light. I never thought to complain.

After a few months, my parents decided to have the front bedroom, my grandparents' room, divided in two. My grandparents would move to my parents' room. My parents would move into Andy's room at the back of the house. Since Andy had had a private room and his own bathroom for all these years, I would be given the larger of the two new rooms. The green and yellow bathroom would be mine.

I couldn't wait for the work to be finished. The workmen seemed to be in the house forever, but at last they had installed two new doors, closets, and a dividing wall, and departed.

Mother and I went downtown to look for wallpaper. At the wallpaper store I saw some with a dark smoky blue background. Luxurious bouquets of yellow and white roses were scattered across the blue. Mother tried to convince me that it was too dark and dramatic, but it was the one I wanted. Finally she purchased the necessary rolls. She and my father hung the paper, as they had done throughout the house.

Mother made white café curtains and a white ruffle for my new vanity table. Our neighbor in the next house down the hill, Mrs. Start, gave me a pair of antique mirrors, oval, with carved gilt frames. We hung them side-by-side above the vanity. I was given a small table to use as a desk and, at Christmas, a tall chest of drawers. I helped select two lamps, white china with painted bouquets of flowers.

When the household changed rooms, the beds remained in place where they had always been. My parents had purchased my bed, formerly used by Miss C. and then by my grandparents, in an antique shop in Omaha. Some pioneer had made it for his bride. He had carved and turned elaborate bedposts and railings from walnut. It was wide but shorter than modern beds. I had always admired it. I was pleased that its heavy white chenille bedspread matched my new décor.

I was altogether delighted with my pretty room. I hadn't realized the pleasures of privacy. How good it was to have my own door to close. Now I was glad my parents didn't want to share their room with me anymore.

My single mattress and frame went to my brother. He thought the pineapples on the mahogany posts too girlish, so my bed remained in the attic. My parents thought this new arrangement was fair, so he didn't dare to make more than a token complaint about his diminished space and comfort.

First thing every Saturday morning, it was my job to clean my new room and bath. It was a pleasure to arrange and rearrange my things behind a closed door. There I was free to make small decisions on my own: where to put my comb and brush, whether the box of apple blossom body powder should be on my vanity or on my dresser, which dolls to put on my bed. I'd seldom had the opportunity to decide anything. These exercises of autonomy were something very special — choosing wallpaper, arranging my things.

Saturday mornings were especially enjoyable on stormy days. With rain or wind beating against the windows, I could indulge in delicious melancholy, pretending to be marooned and alone with my dolls, my body powder, and my double reflection in the gilt mirrors.

One of my windows looked out over Cliff Street. An enormous silver maple tree grew on one side of our short front walk and a huge elm on the other. On summer nights, as the white curtains blew against the screen, I listened to the creak and rub of the trees and the rustle of their leaves. In the winter, with the windows closed, I could hear the shriek of cold wind through bare branches.

The tree sounds made them seem almost like people. I still miss their company.

I continued to "roll and sing" until the day I began ninth grade. I had long felt embarrassed by this peculiar habit, but had been unable to stop. I thought reviewing my day in song helped my memory. I believed I could remember every significant thing I had seen or done since the age of two. As I formed my stories into song, I continued to imagine some amorphous someone listening to them.

However, on this morning I said to myself that continuing this bizarre behavior meant no man would ever marry me. Besides, why did I need to remember everything? Why was it important?

I quit. It was extremely difficult. I fought my compulsion for months, but I never again succumbed to its lure. Over the years, my memory has gradually deteriorated, especially about events since ninth grade.

14 ❖ Wary of Love

Burlington, 1944–1948

Andy had always wanted a pet. Neither of my parents had ever had a pet. My mother's family had been too poor and had moved too often. My father's family had been too meticulous and concerned about their furniture.

My parents would have been glad to continue pet-less. However, my brother had dealt with so many difficulties in his life—his third round of rheumatic fever, months and months of missed school, and our several moves—that my parents decided to grant him this indulgence. Andy's first choice was a dog, but when he was told that a dog was out of the question, he was glad to settle for a cat.

So when I was about four and Andy about nine, we acquired a cat. Our cat, named Kitty, as in "Here Kitty, Kitty, Kitty," was not given a litter box. I'm not sure they were in common use in the forties. He learned to meow at the door when he wished to go outside and to meow at the door when he wanted to come back in. He was also not neutered. Consequently Kitty roamed.

Cliff Street had little traffic, but South Union at the foot of our block and South Willard at the head were busy thoroughfares. When Kitty disappeared and didn't return after a couple of days, my parents told us he had "run away." As far as I remember, they made no inquiries as to his welfare or whereabouts.

Andy and I continued to watch for him. We both missed him. I liked to pet Kitty, when he permitted it, and to watch him eat and wash his paws, and to listen to him purr, but I admired him more than I had loved him. I knew he was Andy's cat. When Kitty seemed even to us to be gone for good, we pushed hard for another cat.

Our parents inquired around and soon a new kitten came to take the place of the missing Kitty. This was a little female, a yellow and white tiger we also called Kitty.

Mother showed us how to prepare a thin gruel of Pablum and warm milk. We put it in a shallow saucer on a newspaper we laid down over the green-and-black linoleum squares in a corner of the kitchen. We placed the kitten in front of the saucer.

She sniffed frantically, but didn't seem to have any idea what to do next. Andy guided her little head into the milk mixture. She pulled back, sneezing violently, shaking her whiskers, as tiny spatters of Pablum and milk flew in all directions. Andy tried again and then again with no better success. Kitty was now standing in the saucer, sneezing, milk and Pablum matting down the fur of her four legs.

At last we saw her pink tongue curl in her first attempts to lap up the gruel. When the mess was in her small stomach, now round and hard—at least the part of the mess that wasn't dripping from her legs and chin—Andy lifted her out of the saucer. She sat beside it, getting another meal as she licked her fur clean, washing her face with her curled paws as though she were a grown-up cat.

I was enchanted. From that day on, I loved Kitty extravagantly. She grew up to be patient and friendly, rubbing against my legs and jumping on my lap. I soon considered her to be *my* cat. I petted her and carried her around, draped around my neck or cuddled in my arms. I was no longer so afraid of the poisoners in the closet or the man beneath my bed, because I brought Kitty upstairs with me at night. I put her under my covers to feel her crawl and play her way down my body, until she pounced at my bare feet. Kitty was the first thing I looked for in the morning and the last thing I said good night to in the evening.

But unknown to me, Kitty had her own separate existence and her own destiny to fulfill. Kitty began to act very strangely. She meowed incessantly, rubbed herself against the living room carpet, was too restless to let me hold her, and begged at the door to be let out. Then she was gone for longer periods of the day and wouldn't come in at night. One morning she wasn't waiting to be let in. She didn't appear that day or that evening. The next morning again there was no sign of her.

I could not be comforted. I loved her too much for it to be possible that she would leave me. My parents tried to assure me that she would be back, and I tried to believe them. On the third day there was still no sign of Kitty. I was so frantically unhappy that my father went out looking for her.

He came back without her and immediately sat down at the desk in the front hall to telephone the Humane Society. I waited on the staircase, listening.

"Has anyone reported finding a yellow tiger cat, female, full grown, in the vicinity of Cliff Street? No? Yes, I'll wait," he looked over at me and smiled. He tapped his broad fingers on the desk. "Oh, Oh, I see." He stopped smiling. "Well, thank you. At least now we know."

My father told me two days before someone had reported a dead cat in the middle of South Union Street. It was a yellow tiger, a female.

It wasn't Kitty. It couldn't be Kitty.

My father said he was afraid it must be our cat.

Could we get her? Could we see for sure? Could we bring her home?

No, she was gone. They didn't have her any more. And my father was sure I wouldn't want to see her dead anyway.

Dead. Dead. Dead meant never moving again, never purring. I would never hold her again. I thought wildly there must be a way to bring her back. She couldn't be gone. How could something be alive one minute, then still forever after? How could something I loved be gone forever? How could something I loved be gone at all?

When my shock and disbelief wore off a little, I began a wild sobbing that I couldn't stop. First my father and then my mother tried to calm me down, but I couldn't be comforted. Finally they sent me upstairs to cry it out in private. I cried there in absolute black despair.

When I finally came downstairs, my brother said to me, "It's your fault Kitty got run over. You made her run away because you picked her up all the time. She wanted to get away from *you!*" My mother told him that wasn't a nice thing to say, but I worried that maybe it was true and began to cry all over again.

Two things resulted from the pain of that day. Never since have I abandoned myself so unrestrainedly to love. Never since have I been caught so unprepared for the blankness and finality of death. Having realized that anything can end, end unexpectedly and end forever, I have held a little bit of myself back in readiness for the loss that waits just out of sight. I never let myself go.

A few months after Kitty was killed, one early August afternoon in 1946, I was playing in the backyard of a house up near the top of our street when I heard my father whistle. His whistle was powerful enough to be heard indoors or outside anywhere in the block where, now that I was five-and-a-half years old, I was permitted to roam. It usually summoned us home for our meals. But so early in the afternoon, his two-note call had previously meant only one thing: either my brother or I or both had done something bad and were being called home for a spanking. Frightened, I ran down the hill trying to think what I might have done wrong this time.

When I scurried up the steps of the front porch, there indeed was Mother, her face very serious, holding open the door for me. As I stepped inside, however, I saw only my father's shaking back. He was sitting at the desk, his arms folded upon it, his face resting on his arms. He didn't turn around or move when I came through the door.

Mother put her finger to her lips and beckoned me into the living room. She walked me to the corner by the fireplace and whispered, "Granddaddy Nuquist was killed in an automobile accident this morning. Your daddy just got the call from Nebraska."

I felt only a strange blankness. Granddaddy and Grandmother had come to visit us a few weeks before. Granddaddy had joked with us a little, but I was too big now to sit on his lap and listen to the tick-tick of his pocket watch. He wasn't nearly as interesting as he had been when we visited in Nebraska. He walked very slowly using a cane. When we went to the garden for our dinners, my brother had to bring Granddaddy one of our straight white kitchen chairs. He could no longer bend well enough to get in and out of the garden chairs. Granddaddy dropped a tiny white pill in his coffee instead of a spoonful of sugar. He wasn't supposed to eat Mother's cherry cobbler. After meals he dozed in my father's big brown plush chair in the living room.

I thought about these things and waited to feel the crushing sadness I had experienced when I had heard about Kitty's being dead. It didn't come. I didn't feel much of anything.

I was dismayed. What would Daddy think? He was so sad. How could I not be sad too? I didn't want him to know I wasn't feeling sad enough to cry, so I squeezed out some tears. Not many came. I decided the best thing to do was once again to rush upstairs to my room, pretending to cry and to feel the way I had when Kitty died. I hoped that would make Daddy feel better. I tried to act sad until Daddy left the next day to take the train to Nebraska.

Even then I tried to understand why I suffered so much more about my Kitty than about Granddaddy Nuquist. I couldn't understand it, however, and was left only with my guilt about the difference. I knew I was *supposed* to love him more.

When the next kitten came into the house later that fall, I had become a different person, more wary of love and its complications. Blackie was a nice cat, and I enjoyed her very much, but I kept a little distance. Mother assisted with my relative detachment.

The first time Blackie had kittens, Andy and I were charmed and delighted. For six weeks we watched the kittens grow, gave them names and played with them by the hour. Mother agreed with us that they were adorable, but reminded us that we couldn't keep them. If we couldn't find them homes, they would have to go to the Humane Society. She had a suggestion for us, however. Since the kittens were so very cute why didn't we choose one of them to keep and send off the mother?

We were horrified, but, oh, it was a terrible temptation. Eventually we succumbed. I felt sickening guilt and disloyalty the day my father drove off with three kittens and Blackie. She meowed and tried to get out of the car although innocent of the fate to which we had consigned her.

After that we always traded in the old cat for the new kitten. Each time I found the struggle with my heart and conscience easier. I still enjoyed the cats, petted them, played with them, liked to watch them, and took them to bed with me, but my relationship to the cats was more casual, and my sense of responsibility to them diminished. So young and already cruel and callous.

I was to find many opportunities in the future to yield to suggestions against my better judgment.

15 ❖ The Campaign

Vermont, 1946

In 1946 Daddy ran for Congress in the Republican primary. Vermont was a Republican-controlled state. It conducted a two-party election but everyone knew the only election was the primary. So to my Grandmother Nuquist's horror, Daddy entered the race as a Republican.

During the campaign Congressman Charles Plumley, the incumbent, gave a speech in which he told the audience that some of his friends supported the proposed bounty on beavers, while some others of his friends were opposed to such a measure. And where did he stand on the merits of the issue? "I'm for my friends," said Charlie.

My father had been approached by a group of prominent men who thought it was well past time for a change. "I can't afford a campaign," my father told them. "How much do you need?" they asked. "Five thousand dollars," he answered, and it was provided.

My mother gave up her position as president of the Burlington League of Women Voters to manage my father's campaign. She had no experience running a campaign, but my father had long depended upon her organizational skills. My father worried that he was still considered a newcomer to the state, a flatlander, having lived in Vermont for only eight years, and he had the misfortune of teaching at the university. He had overheard people say he must be Jewish because of his thin beak of a nose and his strange name.

The five thousand dollars provided for printing and distributing cards, posters, and advertisements for the newspapers and the radio stations. Daddy's posters said he was "Independent, Youthful, Informed, Awake" and promised "sober consideration of all legislation." Congressman Plumley was reported to like his liquor and perhaps as a consequence often would fall asleep during deliberations. He was certainly not young.

The money purchased a used pre-World War II car that carried us from one campaign appearance to the next. Its frequent failure made my father late for many events. The radiator overheated; fan belts and hoses disintegrated; the headlights failed.

One night after the car broke down again we all stood beside a dark empty road. I remember the oncoming lights and roar of a bus. My father stepped into the road, waving his brown felt fedora like a signal flag. The bus rumbled to a stop. My brother and I stumbled up the stairs, Mother close behind, into the curving gray plush interior, the few sleepy, curious faces roused momentarily by the row of lights the driver had turned on for us.

My father remained with the car. His ghostly white shirt disappeared as the bus pulled away. In the bus every snore, whispered conversation, scent of dust and tobacco was intensified by a new phrase, "unscheduled stop," and a new hour, midnight. The silent driver stared ahead into the darkness, his face a waxy candle lit by the glow from his cigarette.

I don't know when or how my father got home. I don't remember the long dark walk up the hill from the bus station to our house on Cliff Street.

On another memorable occasion the floor of the car burst into flame. A carpet covering a previously unknown hole beneath the front passenger seat had worked its way down onto the road and friction had turned us into a bonfire. My father, in his good suit, leapt repeatedly over a fence, past startled Jersey cows, and filled one little paper cup after another with water from a fortuitously placed stream until the carpet was sufficiently cool that he could pull the burned remains free and toss them into the ditch beside the road. Mother resumed her seat, her feet placed carefully on either side of the gaping space.

One day we attended a Sunday rally in the Northeast Kingdom of Vermont. We rose early, Mother packed a picnic basket, and we set off on our long drive. A clank and a jolt and something had gone wrong with the car once more. My father got out, raised the hood, and stared helplessly at the engine. His muttered curses rose again and again to audible level. "Now, Andrew," my mother said each time. "Now, Andrew," and he subsided. Finally a farmer came by and patched us up somehow so we could continue, inching forward slowly, while ominous noises rumbled out of the engine.

At last we arrived. Here was something I had never seen—an unpainted farmhouse, torn screens, and a front yard of unmown grass that rose above my knees. Under a tree on a trestle table rested a big jug of lemonade, redolent chicken pot pies, coleslaw, and heaps of fresh strawberries. There was a tethered pony with many children waiting to ride. They knew how to do it! They knew each other.

Mother told us to go play but not to take any food. She said it had been too much work for these women and too much expense for strangers like us to benefit. My father moved off, shaking hands and talking to people. Mother followed him. My ten-year-old brother had become invisible to me. My five-year-old self pressed against the trunk of a tree.

Finally it was time for Daddy's speech. Grown-ups crowded into a dark parlor. Somewhere in the middle of the crowd I sat on Mother's lap. My brother sat beside us. Daddy stood beside the round stove. Everyone looked at him while he talked. I didn't understand what he was talking about but I was so proud. He must be very important. Afterwards we climbed back into the car to begin the creeping, rattling, apprehensive ride home.

Everywhere Daddy spoke—in grange halls, bandstands, living rooms—people applauded. Andy and I were sure he would win, but Mother told us not to get our hopes up. He was running to show that old Charlie was not invincible. That in the *future,* with more time and money, someone would beat him.

Mother gave over managing the campaign to a newspaperman, a convert to the cause with more experience and good connections. Tonight, however, election night, they both thought my father had a chance. The early returns looked good. He was ahead.

Every room on our first floor was crowded with men who clustered around radios, tuned loudly to different stations. Someone sat in the front hall by the telephone that rang again as soon as the receiver was replaced. The house filled with cigarette smoke, the rise and fall of voices, shouts, cheers, oaths, all to the delight of my brother and me. We were at first underfoot, watching the chalked tallies, the slips of paper as they were torn from the adding machine, the men running from room to room with new bits of information. Then we were banished to the top of the stairs where we watched and listened as best we could through the banisters.

This was the most exciting summer of our lives and this, by far, the most exciting evening of all. At midnight our father was ahead. Unbelievably we were both sent to bed. I nursed profound feelings of disappointment and injustice for the five minutes before I fell asleep.

When I awoke the house was quiet. The scent of coffee and bacon had joined the stale odor of cigarettes. I ran downstairs where my parents were moving quietly about. They both looked tired. For a minute I hesitated to ask the question. "I lost," my father said. "I didn't expect to win, you know."

"But you were ahead. You were winning," Andy pleaded.

"I didn't have time to get to every place. I lost where they didn't have a chance to hear me. If I'd gotten into the thing sooner, I might have pulled it off. But I'm still an outsider here."

I felt like crying but I didn't want them to know. I was afraid I would hurt their feelings. I pretended it was nothing much to me, and I didn't ask any more questions.

There was very little further discussion then or ever. I didn't know how my brother felt. He didn't say. Daddy didn't talk about it again, at least not to us. He sold the car as junk. Some time later Mother said she was glad we didn't have to move to Washington. She didn't want to leave our house. She liked Burlington.

Two years later, the same men asked my father to think about another run. They told him that all things considered he did very well. The vote, 31,473 to 23,452, showed the state that Charlie Plumley could be beaten. My father turned them down. He never ran for office again, nor did any other member of the immediate family, but to this day the tallying of any election stirs my blood.

SECTION THREE
Family Album

Junietta Willcuts, circa 1883

Ansalem Jackson, circa 1883

Elizabeth (Bessie), Edith, and
Ruth Jackson, circa 1915

The author at the abandoned Friends Meeting House, Beaver Valley, Neb., 1992

My mother, me (5), Andy (10), and my father,
Burlington, Vt., 1946

Granddaddy Wilson
balancing a broom on his
chin, Earlham, Iowa, 1943

Our hostess Madame Pleger, Solange Biwer,
and, on the right, me flirting with Mickey
at a party in Luxembourg, 1957

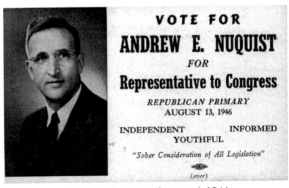

My father's campaign card, 1946

Grandmother Maud, my father Andrew,
and Granddaddy Andrew Nuquist
on the Stantons' porch, Stromsburg, Neb.,
1906

My mother's Penn College
graduation photo, 1928

Grandmother Nuquist,
circa 1944

My mother Edith, Walter, Bessie, Gerald,
Walter's mother, and Donald Wilson, 1918

My Vassar yearbook photo,1962

With Arturo,
Burlington, Vt., June 16, 1962

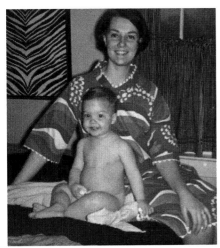

Omar and I,
Stroudsburg, Pa., 1967

Sara in the sunroom,
Burlington, 1972

SECTION FOUR

Love and History

16 ❖ Playing Peter with Grandmother Wilson

Burlington, 1946

It was soon after my father lost his bid for Congress that Granddaddy and Grandmother Wilson came to live with us in Burlington. They moved into the big front bedroom that until then my parents had rented to Miss C.

I visited my grandparents' room all the time. Granddaddy was often away, walking downtown, meeting the neighbors, looking for work, but Grandmother was at home. I "helped" her get settled. I thought their few belongings quite delightful—the little art deco green glass lamp, the pincushion fashioned into the shape of a girl wearing a bonnet, the quilts, and the embroidered pillowcases.

Very soon Grandmother Wilson invented Peter. We played Peter in her room, but Peter came from Grandmother's Nebraska and Iowa childhood when homesteaders were streaming to the prairie from all over the world.

For the game Grandmother transformed herself into Peter's mother, an immigrant from Europe come with her husband to stake a claim and make their fortune. But, alas, now she was a widow, left to struggle on her own in a strange land with only her errant young son Peter to keep her company. Grandmother threw a towel over her head as a make-believe shawl, acquired an accent, and told me stories of Peter's escapades. Peter was a very bad boy who caused his mother a great deal of trouble.

I became whomever she needed to complete the story—Peter's teacher or the constable or the farmer down the road to whom the widow made excuses and explanations.

"I don't know vat I am going to do mit dis boy, your highness constable. Me, a poor vidow voman. He makes me vant to tear out my hair!"

Sometimes I even was Peter, whom she scolded away from the chickens, the apple tree, or the fresh pie. Peter fell into mud puddles climbing over fences or tore his only pants climbing under them. He brought home runts and strays that they couldn't afford to feed.

The game grew ever more elaborate. The room disappeared. I was a little boy running down a dusty road, my mother behind me brandishing a broom. I fell in love with the errant Peter and his mischief, and with his mother, and certainly with my grandmother, who brought me into this wonderful make-believe world.

Then I made the terrible mistake. I invited my friend, Lynne, over to "play Peter." I could see that Grandmother was very embarrassed. She told us she didn't have time. From that moment Peter and his mother disappeared. I was not allowed to talk about them ever again.

"Elizabeth, I don't want you to tell anyone else about Peter."

"I *promise* not to tell anybody. Can't we play Peter today?"

"I'm too old to be playing games. We shouldn't waste our time with such nonsense. I don't want to hear any more about Peter."

Nevertheless, after Peter disappeared, I continued to make my way to Grandmother's room to hear stories about her own youth. I think the past was more interesting to her than what must have been a rather disappointing present, her world shrunk to one upstairs room in her daughter's house.

All her previous life had been spent on the prairies except for the year in Minnesota and four years in Oregon. My grandparents were already long-married and had three children when my grandfather decided to move the family to Newberg, Oregon, to obtain a degree in theology from George Fox College. In 1918 during their stay there Grandmother was trying to feed and clothe her family on Grandfather's part-time income as a supply pastor and as the renter of a small farm. That year she was diagnosed with breast cancer. She was thirty-five years old when her breasts were cut off.

During her recovery, in what must have been excruciating pain, worried about money, her family, and the future, separated from all that was familiar to her, Grandmother suffered a "nervous breakdown." She went home to Nebraska for six months to live quietly with her parents. Her youngest sister, Ruth, sixteen years old, came to Oregon to care for Walter and the children.

Grandmother recovered and returned to her family and its duties, her breasts replaced by a small tablecloth neatly folded and pinned beneath her clothes. Her health and her "nerves" remained fragile. Still, she managed on my grandfather's minuscule income to do what was absolutely necessary to keep her family clothed and fed. She attended first- and fifth-day meetings, and she taught Bible classes. She canned in the summer and even pieced the occasional quilt in the winter, but she was often made weak and ill from the effort.

Now at age sixty-three she faced the daunting task of making new friends and a new life from one upstairs bedroom in her daughter's house. Just before she left Minneapolis, she wrote Mother:

> We certainly did appreciate your letter and the very sensible way you considered our getting on together. We understand it is more *difficult* for two families than one, and we would try to keep to ourselves and do our part. I guess you know that it has been the burden of my heart for years that we get a home or something permanent. Maybe by another year if W. H. finds something he can do we could rent rooms nearby or get a cottage for the summer as caretakers, but just now, after much prayer and waiting, this seems the only way onward, so it must be the right way.

My grandmother never did get something permanent. She and Granddaddy rented an apartment for part of one year, but couldn't continue to pay for it on Granddaddy's uncertain income. They lived at 32 Cliff Street for the rest of their lives.

At 66 Granddaddy still stood on his bald head,
walked on his hands, balanced a broom on his chin
on our small front yard to our delight and Mother's
chagrin.

A job in the Chem Lab where he measured out
acids, crystals and compounds from brown glass
bottles to students too busy to chat. He quit to sell
sidewalk sealer and heavy-duty soap door-to-door.

They remained in the garage despite his daily rounds
downtown, carrying the black sample kit and some of his
five hundred business cards, tipping his hat and greeting
each person he met, standing aside to hold every door.

He swept our porch, our steps, our walk each fine morning.
Spring evenings he planted chard and beets, carrots and kale,
tomatoes and peas, in space he cleared of flowers. After a lifetime
he couldn't allow good land to lie unproductive.

My grandparents ate with us in our dining room when they
were invited, usually once or twice a week for dinner. Otherwise
Grandmother prepared their minimalist meals on her hot-plate or in
my mother's kitchen. They ate on a little table set before the west-
facing window in their room.

Everyone behaved well about this arrangement. I never heard
a single word of complaint from my parents or my grandparents.
My father treated his in-laws with unfailing courtesy and respect.
My mother, although she always turned down my grandfather's
invitations to join in evening games of Chinese checkers or Camelot,
never sounded especially impatient as she did so.

As an adult, I can imagine the daily discipline over tongue and
feelings required from my parents and my grandparents that made
such an arrangement seem desirable in the eyes of an observant child.
I greatly admire them all for that effort.

I'm convinced my mother loved her parents, particularly her
mother, but considered theirs a failed life from which she had nothing
positive to learn. She never said this to me, but over the years I came
to sense her pity for my grandmother and her disappointment with
my grandfather. She certainly never consulted them nor asked for
their advice.

As for me, I was delighted to have live-in grandparents. I enjoyed
their company, particularly my grandmother's, an in-house storyteller
with as much time on her hands as I had. I always felt welcome to
knock on her door. Even when she was occupied with some little
task, dusting or mending or embroidering a tea towel, I could come
in to watch or to "help." Instead of wandering the neighborhood for
stories, now I had only to climb the stairs.

Grandmother Wilson often told me variations of the same stories I
had heard before. I didn't mind. It was like hearing my favorite books
that I wanted read and reread to me as often as possible.

After breakfast I would come upstairs and settle myself cross-
legged on the braided rug next to Grandmother's maple armchair.

**Grandmother Elizabeth (Bessie) Jackson Wilson, 1883–1961,
Burlington, 1947**

The Story I Didn't Tell Elizabeth

I was never a strong woman, sandwiched
between a formidable mother, formidable daughter.
Was I really so weakened at four by my bout
of typhoid fever, or did it become my life-long
excuse? Mostly I managed. There was one time
I didn't cope.

After the cancer and my breasts were removed
that terrible summer of 1918—the ooze and pain,
three small children, the worry about what would
happen to them, about money, Walter's plans that
never seemed to quite work out. I couldn't stop crying,
went home to Mother to rest. Perhaps
I was testing out my absence. Perhaps I wanted
to be gone.

I never gave way like that again but I had to keep
my life very quiet, very calm. My strong-willed
daughter, Edith, took over. She battled the grim
little parsonages we were given with Walter's
churches, made them clean, brought
in flowers, helped me in every way until she
and the boys grew up. She and I were
always good friends although pity is not
a positive, whether given or accepted.

And here I am with Walter in the spare room
of Edith's house. I always had hoped for
a little house of our own, but I am tired now,
used to my quiet ways—content to make most
meals on our little hot plate, to do my daily
devotions, to read the *Reader's Digest*
although my eyes aren't very strong.

My granddaughter knocks on my door
every day and we have good times
together. She likes my stories and,
I'm ashamed to admit, an old lady like me,
my game of make-believe. I pretend we're
back when I was a child, before I was supposed
to *be* anything, the simpler times before
I grew up.

The Story Bessie Did Tell

When I was just one year old, in 1884, Mama and Papa decided to take up a government claim on a section of land in Beaver Valley, Sheridan County, Nebraska, eighteen miles east of Chadron. Papa built us a soddy—that's a house made from blocks of dirt with the grass still growing on the outside—ten feet wide by thirteen feet long, on the banks of Beaver Creek. All we had with us was what would fit on a wagon. Believe you me, we didn't throw away anything.

We had lived in Beaver Creek two years when I got the typhoid. No one else in the family got it, not my little brother Cliff, not my mother who was expecting at the time, not my father. I was so sick they thought for sure I would die. I lost my sense of smell then and it never did come back. I couldn't eat. After sixty some years, I still can't digest rich food. All my hair fell out. It didn't grow back right. You see how thin it is on top. It has been wispy like this ever since. I stayed poorly for months and months and just couldn't seem to get my strength back.

Mother had a new baby to take care of. Life wasn't easy in a soddy even without a sickly little girl to worry about. When I was six, Mother and Father decided I should go to stay for a while with my grandparents back in Iowa. The climate was milder, for one thing, and life was easier. I didn't want to go. My father took me. We got the train at Valentine, but I was too worried to be excited about the ride. The day he left me with Grandmother and Grandfather Jackson I thought I would die for sure.

Grandmother Jackson wore a bonnet and her dresses were plain, and always either gray or brown. My grandparents still said "thee" and "thy." Although they were kind to me and tried to make me feel welcome, they were strict old-time Quakers. They didn't believe in holidays. They said there was too much pagan in them, too much riot and folly. They explained to me that Jesus didn't have a Christmas tree or red bows or special cookies. They didn't approve of Christmas except as an opportunity to gather at a silent meeting for worship.

I knew not to expect any presents or decorations. I knew I mustn't seem sad or ungrateful. I tried not to think about my family having their little Christmas all together in our soddy on Beaver Creek. Imagine how I felt Christmas morning when I woke to discover a doll on my pillow! It was the most beautiful doll I had ever seen and the only bought doll I ever did have. I wish I had it now to show you. She wore a brown dress and a little brown Quaker bonnet that Grandmother had made. The stitches were so tiny I could hardly find them. She had a beautiful porcelain face, porcelain fingers and painted-on black porcelain boots. Grandmother and Grandfather Jackson had given me a Christmas present! After that I always felt in my heart that they loved me best of all. Still to this day I wish I could have stayed with my grandparents. That was the happiest year of my life.

Grandmother was Grandfather's second wife. He had been a widower with nine living children including my father when he married the grandmother I knew, and they had two more children, Aunt Marie and Uncle Ernest. Aunt Marie was still living at home while I was there. She was a grown up young lady. Aunt Marie painted pictures, played the piano, and did beautiful embroidery. I wanted to be accomplished like she was. She tried to teach me to paint and do fine sewing and was so patient with me.

I knew Mother wanted me to be a lady and thought accomplishments were important, even to homesteaders living in sod houses. She would be pleased with me if I learned how to paint and to embroider. She always seemed a little disappointed that I was weak and sickly while she was so strong. In Iowa I still came down with one thing or another and had to rest a lot, but my health did improve there.

The year was up and Papa came to get me. I didn't want to leave. My baby brother, Joe, had gotten big while I was away. He was already walking by the time I first saw him. I helped Mama take care of Cliff and Baby Joe, but there was time to play. With so many relatives living nearby there were many children for me to play with. I was glad that, although I wasn't special the way I was in Iowa, still, everybody knew my name. My father's brother, Uncle Reuben Jackson, had eleven children. Their whole family lived in a one-room soddy too. Every morning they had to move the beds outdoors, and every evening they had to drag them inside again.

While I was away Father had built us our frame house. Mother didn't think sod houses were fit habitations for human beings, so she urged him to build us a real house. Her father, who ran a sawmill back in Iowa, came out to help cut the lumber he had brought with him on the train. Our new house had five rooms. Compared to the soddy, it seemed a palace. My father was always proud to have built the first frame house in Beaver Valley.

We surely didn't stay in it very long, however. Papa never did manage to get a decent crop. He said no matter what people had told him, the land wasn't fit to farm. It was rich enough but you couldn't count on the rain. In 1890 we were very short of money so, much against Papa's wishes, Mama spent a winter in Chadron cooking in a restaurant. Two sisters from the next section, my first cousins, Ada and Minnie Lundy, moved into our new house to take care of us.

That was to be our last year in Sheridan County. The Lundy family stayed because they had enough money to make the switch to ranching. The Reuben Jacksons stayed because they didn't have a choice. My beautiful sister Edith was born in August of 1891. Your mother is named for her, of course. As soon as she was big enough to travel we moved back to Iowa.

Father worked one year in Hardin County at a lumberyard that two of his brothers owned, and then he leased a farm in New Providence. In 1894, when I was eleven years old, we moved back to my Grandfather's house in Hartland, Marshall County. I was so happy to be back in that wonderful house. Grandfather Jackson was seventy-seven years old by then, too old to manage his big farm anymore, so my father took over for him.

I went to a one-room school especially for Gurneyite Quakers. Quakers never could seem to agree for long. There were divisions even among the family. Grandfather and Grandmother were Wilburites, old-fashioned Quakers with silent meetings. Most of us had become Gurneyites with singing and preaching in our meeting and no "thees" and "thys." Then there were the Hicksites. I didn't know much about the Hicksites except they were unsound. Hicksite children went to their own one-room school, and we weren't allowed to talk to or to play with them. When Gurneyite boys met Hicksite boys there were always fights, although Quakers weren't supposed to fight at all of course.

When I finished eighth grade Mother thought I should go to normal school. My father didn't want his daughter boarding with strangers, and he thought eight grades of school were enough for anybody, especially a girl. But my mother talked to him until finally he let me go, and I attended two terms at Cedar Falls Normal School.

I was homesick and discovered I was shy around people I didn't know, but I did enjoy all that I was learning. When I returned to Hartland, I became the teacher in my old school. Because of farm work, many of the boys didn't go to school more than a few months a year. I was sixteen when I began to teach. There were several boys older than I, most of them my cousins. My two younger brothers and my sister Edith were also in my school. It was hard to make them all mind, but I tried to be strong and keep them in some sort of order. I was proud to be earning my own money.

I used some of that money to buy a length of moss-green watered silk. Aunt Marie made the most wonderful dress for me. It had a white lace collar, a very full skirt, and little tucks over the bodice. It was my very first silk dress. How I did admire it. It hung from a hook behind the door to my room. I was so eager for an opportunity to wear it.

That year, like every year, we spent months getting ready for May Day. We girls made the baskets. Each basket was different. Some we patched together out of cloth scraps and then embroidered with daisies and tulips and I don't know what all. Some we wove from strips of all the colored paper we had saved during the year. Some were made from plain paper we painted pictures on and then folded into baskets. Aunt Marie let us copy from a book she had, so we had something special to paint—mountains and waterfalls—instead of plain old corn fields and barns.

We spent the day before May Day hunting wildflowers so that before the sun was up, we were ready to drive out in the wagon. The farms were so far apart it took all day to deliver the baskets.

May Day, the year I got my dress, a terrible storm blew up. A neighbor made us put up the team and come inside, said there was no way he was going to let us be out in all that lightning and thunder. They gave us supper, and when the storm didn't let up, bedded us all down.

In the middle of the night a man rode up calling out the news that the homestead, our wonderful old house, had been hit by lightning and burned to the ground. Everyone had escaped. The house was gone but they were safe. I'm ashamed to tell you that all I could think about that night was my new green dress turning into ashes before I had ever worn it. It was many years before I had another silk dress.

The house was rebuilt, but just as it was completed, Grandfather Jackson died. His properties were sold, and everything was divided among the eleven children. There was some more trouble about that, although I never knew exactly what the problems were. I know Mother didn't think Father got his fair share. My parents decided it was a good time to try the west again, only this time not so far.

In 1902, when I was nineteen, they bought a farm near Central City, Nebraska, and moved there. I stayed behind to finish up my term of teaching and then traveled out alone on the train to join the family. I felt very grown-up. Perhaps that is why I took particular notice of the group of young men, students from Nebraska Central Academy, who had come to see off one of their friends. I was to get to know two of those young men particularly well.

Our farm was near the section of land that had been set aside for the Academy. My brothers and sisters attended some terms at the school, and my mother often invited students to Sunday dinner and to open house in the evenings. I think she knew how much we missed our cousins; maybe she missed having a big family around, too.

Two brothers, Walter and Charley Wilson, came more than anyone because they were pretty much on their own. Their father, a circuit-riding Methodist preacher, died at thirty-two when Walter was four and Charley just two. Their mother, Julia, only twenty-seven when she was widowed, didn't have a family to help her. Her own mother had died when Julia was two. Her father didn't feel he could take care of her. He left her with a family who took her only grudgingly.

She became not much more than a servant to them. She always hoped her father would come back but he never did. Thinking she would always be nothing but a hired girl, she'd been so pleased when Wesley Wilson came courting.

After he died his parents didn't offer her a place in their home. When a German man, a widower with children, asked her to marry him, she did. Her new husband wasn't good to the boys—beat them very hard, very often. They ran away when Walter was fourteen and Charley was twelve. A Quaker farmer, Fred Marsh, took them in. He was so kind and fair to them that they became Quakers, too.

After they finished their morning farm chores at the Marshes, Charley and Walter went early to the academy to carry in coal, light the fire, fill and clean the lamps, shovel snow, or do whatever else was required. They stayed after to sweep up. That way they could go to school since otherwise, they couldn't pay the fees.

Charley was a wonderful boy. Everybody loved him. He could make anyone happy just being near him. He was smart and handsome. We loved to be teased by him. Charley came to Sunday dinner one day like always, and I was glad to see him like always. The next day he took sick. Three days later he was dead—appendicitis. Nineteen years old. I could hardly believe it.

Walter broke down at the funeral. I felt so bad for him. Charley and Walter had been together practically every minute, and now Walter was left all alone. After awhile Walter and I started keeping company. I taught in a grammar school in Central City for a few terms and then on July 25, 1906, Walter and I were married in the parlor at the farm. I made my dress—white cotton lawn.

It's strange. I hardly ever speak about Charley any more, and yet after all these years I can see him as clear as though he were standing right here between us.

17 ❖ Bessie's Mother and Father

Great-Grandmother Junietta Willcuts Jackson, 1865–1947
Great-Grandfather Ansalem C. Jackson, 1855–1937

Great-Grandfather was twenty-six, a quiet, steady sort of man, when he asked Joseph Wilcutts's permission to marry his sixteen-year-old daughter, Junietta. According to legend, the reply was, "Take her, take her! I've never been able to do a thing with her. Perhaps you'll have better luck!"

I'm not sure he did, exactly, but there is no doubt his life was more interesting than it might otherwise have been.

It was Junietta, the blind pie-maker I met when she was seventy-nine and I was three, who convinced Ancie, as she called him, to homestead in Nebraska in 1884 on land recently appropriated from the Lakota. Of course this is the story as she told it, but no one contradicted her. It's possible no one *ever* contradicted her.

Junietta's story

I know I was a handful
but I could never think
that was a bad thing. Someone
had to step up, step out,
take a stand, get things done.
I always had the energy,
I always had the strength.
Ancie knew what he was getting
(and between you and me, he
liked what he got).

In my memory there were always Indians. Right from the first they were friendly. They would turn their ponies out in our pasture, walk right into the house. They bought bread and butter of us. Lots of times they ate at our table. They came to pick fruit along Beaver Creek. That fruit—wild plum, gooseberry, and chokecherry—was important to us, too. I put by jellies and jams that lasted us the year. I would be picking right beside the Indians. When fruit is ripe, no matter how much you pick, there is always more than a body can use, so I was glad to share.

After all, my name came from a poem about an Indian girl. "Wild rowed an Indian girl, bright Alfaretta / where sweep the waters of the blue Junietta / Swift as an antelope through the forest going / Loose were her pretty locks in wavy tresses flowing." Once we got to Beaver Valley, though, I don't remember ever seeing an Indian with wavy hair.

Ancie and I and little Bessie, just a year old, settled on homestead land in the valley in 1884. I was eighteen and Ancie was twenty-eight, and we had already been married for two years when we took the train from our home in Marshall County, Iowa, to the end of the line: Valentine, Nebraska. Then we traveled a week by wagon until we came to our claim on Beaver Creek, fourteen miles north of Hay Springs, just two miles north of the Spotted Tail Indian Agency and a mile or so from old Camp Sheridan and the Sheridan Gates. Both the Agency and Camp Sheridan closed in 1877, when the Indians were forced onto reservations, and the buildings were torn down in 1881, three years before we arrived.

The road up from Hay Springs, narrow and dangerous to wagons, winds through stands of ponderosa and chalky buttes, following, the best way it can, twisted creek bottoms. Although I never saw the body or the bones, the story was that Crazy Horse, after he was stabbed to death at Fort Robinson, was placed on a burial scaffold just east of that road in the wild country between Hay Springs and our claim.

Just beyond Camp Sheridan and the Sheridan Gates, twin buttes that marked the road for early travelers, the land flattened out, and it was there Beaver Creek cut through the southwest corner of our land. A dense tangle of wild plum and gooseberry bushes and a few tall cottonwoods grew down along its banks. From that point our land rose gradually to the buttes that formed a wall far to the east. Ancie and his brother and brothers-in-law built our little sod house, ten-by-thirteen feet, near the road, just above the creek bank to the north. We could hear the water running and the cottonwood leaves rustle in the prairie wind.

Ancie was from a very large family, one of eleven living children. One of his brothers and two of his sisters and their husbands homesteaded in the valley with us. We were all members of the Society of Friends — Quakers. At first we held meeting in our homes, but then Ancie's brother-in-law, Dan Lundy, gave a little corner of Section 33, his land on the road to Chadron, as a site for a meeting house. It was a beautiful piece of prairie ground, high enough we could see trouble coming from any direction.

We bought a saloon building the cowboys had run on the big ranch in the center of the valley, tore it down, and used the boards to build our meeting house. I always thought the Lord must be pleased about that.

The Oglala thought all this land was theirs to use, even after a few of their chiefs sold it in 1877 and agreed to move to a reservation on the Missouri. Some bands never did leave, hiding out among the pines and buttes, hunting what game was left and picking wild fruit. Grieving and dying in a strange land along the Missouri, the Oglala were allowed to return to Pine Ridge Agency in 1884, the year we came to Nebraska.

We tried to do all we could for them. I doctored their sick children, and I tried to teach them how to treat their wives better. I made the men let their wives sit down and eat with them at our table. The men didn't enjoy that even a little bit. I've seen a husband hitch two squaws in front of the ponies by a rope, and then get back in the wagon while the women pulled it up the steep hill out of our creek bottom.

John Shut-the-Door and his wife and little son, Sure Shot, became our special friends the years we stayed in Beaver Valley. He was a Christian and used to sing hymns for us. He was a good singer and could write, too.

Looking back, it's not hard to see why we feared an uprising. In 1889 there had been no harvest to speak of. Whatever wasn't eaten by grasshoppers had withered and turned to dust in the hot prairie winds. As bad as 1889 was for us, it was worse for the Indians. The government issued them musty flour and old Texas Ranger beef that wasn't fit to eat. Anyways, the herd mostly died off from anthrax before the Indians got the chance to try. Any game that didn't die in the drought was hunted down by ranchers and the farmers who weren't getting a crop. In August General George Crook and the Sioux Land Commission managed to finagle nine million acres of the best cattle range just north of our land away from the Sioux.

All fall and winter we heard rumors about strange doings among the Indians—that they were dancing for days and nights at a time and no one could stop them. They were singing that their dead would rise again. But all white people would die. Everyone called it "Ghost Dancing."

We asked our friend, John Shut-the-Door, about it. He said the Indians were sharing the words of Wovoka, a Paiute thought by many to be a messiah. Wovoka had seen a vision of a great flood of mud and water that would kill all whites but not Indians who prepared in time. If the Indians danced hard enough, they would be lifted up over the floodwaters and held there until the waters went down. Wovoka said the earth would be alive again, new and green with young grass, and the elk, antelope, and even the buffalo would return.

John Shut-the-Door told us that Kicking Bear, a Minneconjou chief, was reminding his people that when the first messiah came, whites tortured and killed him, and any Indian could see that white hearts had not been made over. This time the Indian messiah would ride a whirlwind and whites would melt like winter snow before him.

There were a number of squaw men, Frenchmen who had married Indian women, living in Beaver Valley. They were uneasy. They told everyone that the Indians were planning an outbreak after the moon that marked the time when grass would be tall enough for ponies to live on. At first everyone just laughed because most of the poor old Indians seemed so worn down and worn out. But the rumors were everywhere, on every corner in Hay Springs and Rushville, in the papers, until people began to think maybe there was something in all the talk after all. The women, especially, began to be nervous and to think and talk about their safer homes back east.

Almost in the center of the valley was the headquarters of the Cowgill Ranch. Twenty-five men took care of four thousand head of cattle and five hundred horses. Their house was a one-story log building, eighty feet long and thirty feet wide. As the fever of fear grew, it was decided that we could all go to the ranch if the Indians did go on the warpath.

On the night of June 15th, we were awakened from deep sleep.

"Hello there!"

Ancie jumped to the window. "Who's there? What is wanted?"

It was John Reno, a young man, none too brilliant, who lived on the road the Indians traveled a great deal, close to the agency line. His voice was all a-quivering.

"The Indians have broke out and are coming this way! The agent has sent word for all settlers to gather at the ranch. Protect yourselves as best you can!"

At this news I was just paralyzed. What were we to do? Our horses were in pasture a half-mile from the house. The ranch was a mile and a half away. We couldn't run on foot there with our three little children.

Ancie tried to calm me down. "Oh, I don't believe it. I don't believe they will come down here even if they do break out. Let's stay here until daylight, anyway."

But I was almost scared to death. My teeth chattered and at first my limbs shook so I couldn't stand. I'd heard that Indians always done their worst work just at break of day.

"No!" I said. "We will go now! You get the horses. I'll stay here with the children."

Oh, such an hour as I went through, expecting the Indians to fall upon us at any moment. I could almost see them. I was afraid to make a light. I cried and wailed, waited and cried, but somehow I fumbled around in the dark and found enough clothes to dress us all. I had the children ready when Ancie came with the team.

When we did get started, we could hear people from every direction driving like mad. Needless to say, we did the same. It was about three o'clock in the morning when we reached the ranch. And such a sight!

Everyone within a radius of six or seven miles was there. Wagons lined up on every side; lanterns hung everywhere; the yard full of armed men. Some carried rifles that had not been used since their coming to the country. There were shotguns, revolvers, corn knives, clubs—every possible weapon anybody could think of.

The men were walking up and down the yard in the lantern light, good targets, bragging to each other about how they were good and ready to kill Indians.

Inside the ranch house, the floor was filled with sleeping children. The women were as pale as death, some speechless, some wringing their hands and crying. "What will we do?" "We'll all be killed at daylight." "Oh, I wish I had never come to this heathen country!"

Some people took time to dress. They put on their best and brought their valuables with them. Others came in nightclothes, barefoot, no shoes or stockings. Parents had lifted their sleeping children, bed and all, into a lumber wagon and brought them as they were. Others brought flour, meat, and provisions to last a week. Most people brought nothing.

There we waited. Hours passed. Someone thought to inquire where the story started, and how, and to ask who got the word from the agency. No one knew anything except that John Reno had ridden by with the message.

Finally two or three of the bravest men and best riders in the valley volunteered to ride to the Agency. If they could escape the Indians and get through, they would find out the truth of the matter. Kissing their wives and children good-bye, away they rode into the very jaws of death. By hard riding they could be back by nine or ten in the morning—if they ever did come back.

They did. More disgusted men never lived. When they reached the agency at daylight, all was quiet. No one was astir. There was no outbreak, no trouble. The Indians were quietly asleep in their tents.

John Reno had heard several loads of Indians go by in the night—Indians did most of their traveling by night. They were making a great deal of noise. It must be the long-talked-about outbreak. Away he rode to give the alarm without stopping to investigate. As the story spread it grew, as stories always do.

We all went back to our several places of abode, thinking we were glad it was as it was, and thankful we saw no Indians as we rode.

The next week after this scare, Ancie's brother, Jim Jackson, and his wife Lou arrived in Beaver Valley from Iowa. They traveled in a covered wagon, having crossed both the Standing Rock and Pine Ridge Indian Reservations without getting into any trouble. Jim was bothered by a weakness of the lungs and he and Lou thought an extended time in the out-of-doors might be just the ticket to clear up his trouble. They planned to travel all the way to Yellowstone Park.

By the time they reached us, we had made all the necessary arrangements so we could go with them, renting out our house and land to a young man who was trying to save up capital for a place of his own. He was to take care of the animals and mind the crops over the summer. For payment, he was to have half of our harvest.

I had a time persuading Ancie that it was the right thing to do, but I kept telling him we were both young and strong, the children were well, and when would another chance like this ever come along? We left Bessie and Cliff and Little Joe with Sarah and Dan Lundy whose place was on the section just to the west of ours. Sarah and Dan had two children of their own, Gertrude and Claude, plus Ada and Minnie, Dan's grown daughters by his first wife.

The four of us rode out of the valley in two covered wagons, each pulled by a team of two horses. In addition, Ancie brought along our riding pony tied to the back of our wagon. We were gone three months and never was in a house to sleep the whole time. Altogether we traveled almost three thousand miles. We took provisions with us. Most days while Lou and I set up camp, Jim and Ancie would hunt or fish. They got enough that we could trade trout or whitefish, sage hens or grouse, for flour or coffee or eggs with settlers or travelers we met up with as we rode along. Lou and I picked gooseberries and raspberries. We baked beans and bread over our campfire.

We crossed two Indian reservations and spent over two weeks on the Crow lands. We didn't have any trouble with the Indians. They were friendly, but all knew about the trouble at Pine Ridge. The Crow and Cheyenne hated the Sioux. Indians would come visit us where we had made camp almost every night and would stay until bedtime. One night, after we were asleep, some young bucks stole our horses, but they didn't take them very far. In the morning Jim and Ancie soon found them, and, after a lot of talking and a little money, we got our horses back. We thought of it as a kind of tax for traveling through their lands.

The Crow were the richest Indians we ever knew. They had lots of fine land and ponies. They took all their ponies, their dogs and their families to the agency twice a month to get government rations. We visited their schools and hospitals, mostly run by Catholics, but some by the government who employed others besides Catholics.

We arrived at the edge of Yellowstone Park on July 20, 1890. At Cinnabar City, the end of the railroad, we watched passengers leave the trains and get on coaches drawn by six or eight fine horses. They rolled by in fine state on their way to Mammoth Hotel, but there were plenty of folks roughing it just like us. Altogether we spent nine days touring the park. By night the mosquitoes and by day the gnats about carried us off. Otherwise we had ourselves a time.

Our return trip was more or less the same as the trip out, although moseying along the way we done, there was always somebody new to meet up with for a few miles or even to camp beside. But we arrived home to all sorts of trouble.

Another dry hot summer meant there weren't going to be any crops to divide; there wasn't even going to be a harvest. We didn't know how we were going to last through the winter or what we would plant in the spring. There was still talk of an Indian war, rumors as bad as when we left.

Over the summer the government had cut the beef issue again and had sent out an order that Indians couldn't hunt game even on their own reservations. While Ancie and Jim had been provisioning us with birds and fish, the Indians living on the lands we were crossing weren't allowed to do the same. The story was that even Indians who hadn't been dancing were leaving the agency in protest and were gathering in camps near the Ghost Dancers.

I got busy picking whatever wild plums and gooseberries there were. For the first time no Indian women picked beside me, not even John Shut-the-Door's wife. I didn't like the feel of that.

The news in the *Chadron Democrat* made us even more nervous:

November 20, 1890

Troops F, I, and K of the 9th cavalry, and Company C of the 8th Infantry, stationed at Ft. Robinson, passed through Chadron yesterday at noon, enroute to Rushville, at which point troops from Ft. Omaha and Ft. Niobrara have also massed, and seven companies from Ft. D.A. Russell, Wyo. are expected also. The object of the marshalling of these troops is to put a stop to the Indian ghost dance that has been the cause of so much trouble upon the different agencies during the past eight or nine months. The government is taking the proper course in putting a stop to these orgies, for instead of their enthusiasm abating with time, as

it was supposed in the beginning it would, it continues to grow, and
if left unchecked, there is no telling where it might end, as the leaders
of the new religion have grown insolent and defy the authority of the
agent on matters pertaining to the regulation of the agency, and it is this
state of affairs that should not be allowed to exist. There is no need of
any scare, as the troops are ready at an easy distance of Pine Ridge, and
there is little doubt but their presence will of itself bring the Indians
to a proper sense of their condition and duty, but if it should be found
necessary to administer them a wholesome chastisement, this is just the
time of year to do it.

November 27, 1890
A sermon preached by the Messiah's prophet, Short Bull,
October 31, 1890 at the Rosebud Agency:

*We must dance the balance of this moon, at the end of which time the earth
will shiver very hard. Whenever this occurs, I will start the wind. We will
then see our fathers, mothers, and everybody. We, the Indians, are the ones
who are living a sacred life. Our father in heaven has placed a mark at each
end of the four winds—a clay pipe lies at the setting of the sun, representing
the Arapahoe tribe, at the south there lies a pipe and a feather, representing
the Crow tribe. My father has shown me these things and we must continue
the dance. There may be soldiers surround you but pay no attention to them;
continue to dance. If the soldiers surround you four deep, three of you upon
whom I have put my holy shirts will sing a song I have taught you and some
soldiers will drop dead. The rest will run, but their horses will sink into the
earth. The riders will jump but they will sink into the earth and you can do
what you desire. Now, you must know this, that all the soldiers and the white
race will be dead. There will only be 5,000 of the living on the earth. My
friends and relations this is straight and true. We must gather at the Pass creek
when the tree is sprouting; then it will go among our relations. You must not
take any things with you. Men and women will disrobe themselves. My Father
above has told us this is so. Guns are the only thing we are afraid of, but our
Father will see that they do us no harm. Whatever the white men say do not
listen to them.*

When the troops came, things just got all the more stirred up at Pine Ridge. The Indians said that every time soldiers had come before, they had attacked, even peaceful camps. So, worried about their women and children, many slipped away with them to the Ghost Dance. But then the soldiers decided that they had to break up the Ghost Dance camps and make the Indians go back to the agencies.

December 11, 1890

'Turn loose the dogs of war.' North and South Dakota, Nebraska, Wyoming, and Montana will soon be supplied with one thousand guns each with which to fight Indians. Now if the government will adopt a new style of gun—something that can be loaded with beef, flour, and bacon, and then the whole five thousand discharged in the direction of Bad Bull's camp over in the vicinity of Wounded Knee, the Indian trouble would soon be over.

On December 14, Sitting Bull was killed by Indian police sent to arrest him by Agent McLaughlin at Standing Rock. After that, almost everyone expected trouble.

The settlers and the soldiers, too, thought the Sioux holed up in the Badlands with the Ghost Dance leaders would want revenge for the death of their chief. People got ready for war. Men went off to Pine Ridge and were sworn for duty.

Since we were Quakers, Ancie didn't want anything to do with shooting, but he hired out to the government to drive a four-mule ambulance wagon. They put him to work taking officers and high hats back and forth to the railhead at Rushville, twenty-five miles from the Agency. He had been at Pine Ridge about a week when the Seventh Cavalry was sent out to round up Big Foot's band camped on Wounded Knee Creek. Big Foot had agreed to surrender there.

At nine o'clock in the morning of December 29, 1890, Ancie and everyone else at Pine Ridge began to hear steady gunfire. By noon, almost all the friendly Indians living at the Agency packed up and fled away north in the direction of the Ghost Dance camps. Later in the afternoon, when most of the sounds of faraway guns had stopped, warriors gathered on a hilltop and began firing on the town. Ancie said the Sioux howled like wild coyotes while they raced their ponies down into the agency, firing their guns, and then raced back up the hills. Ancie said the screaming got into your blood, but no one was hurt, and after a while the Indians rode off.

That night Ancie helped unload the dead and wounded. They brought back twenty-five dead soldiers and thirty-four more wounded. They also brought back more than thirty Indian squaws and children. Ancie said the wounds were terrible, both the soldiers and the Indians cut to pieces. There were questions about what could cause injuries like that except our big revolving cannons with their explosive shells, the Hotchkiss guns. Since only we had Hotchkiss guns, how did our own soldiers get shot by them?

Two days later a burial party went out, mostly Indians organized by a young Indian doctor at the agency, Dr. Eastman, who had been taking care of the Indian wounded, but a few whites went along. They found dead Indians—men, squaws, and children—scattered around in the snow as far as three miles away from the campsite. A big circle of bodies was found in front of Big Foot's tent that was still flying a white surrender flag, now all frozen and ripped by bullets. The Indians said there were three hundred bodies, but the whites didn't count them before they dumped them in a big burial ditch.

Many of the bodies were naked because the soldiers had stripped them for souvenirs—Ghost shirts, weapons, moccasins, baby clothes. They exhibited the things in different places. The bank in Chadron put on display in its window the Ghost shirt and other things taken off a dead brave. I saw them there—all torn up by bullets and covered with blood.

But in the meantime, the day after the shooting, with Indians fleeing in every which way, it was thought for sure they would come to our valley and attack us. The military sent word we were to go at once to Chadron.

When that word came, I was away from home. A neighbor woman was confined and since there wasn't anyone else to do it, I had become the doctor in Beaver Valley for such cases. Poor Alice was in full labor with her first baby. She wasn't fit to be moved, nor could I leave her. The children were with the Lundys. I could only hope the Lundys had got word and that my children were safe with them in Chadron.

What a night that was. Every time the wind blew or a branch creaked, we were sure the Indians were upon us. Alice's husband sat with a gun in his hand, while Alice and I labored and prayed. But by morning there was a new baby. Quite a birthday for that little girl.

I rode home, looking over my shoulder as I went. I found everyone gone. My brother-in-law had left a note for me that they had taken the children to town. We had a new house by then, some cattle, and almost three hundred and sixty acres of land. Didn't I just hate to leave, but leave I must, so I got my team ready again and away I drove the eighteen miles to Chadron, expecting to be set upon every mile.

Where were the children, I worried, and of course, I didn't know what had become of Ancie nor he of us. The agency had been put under martial law and no one could go in or out. In Chadron I found everyone just piled in anywhere they could — into churches, stores, the town hall, and people's houses. It was a new town and the buildings were small — dirty snow and frozen mud, horses, militiamen, and people looking scared to death.

I finally found my family crowded into a little four-room house with two other families. There were beds everywhere, children down with catarrh, whooping cough, and our own people sick from colds they had taken on the ride to town. I stayed two days. By the end of the second day, I decided I might just as well go home and see to things.

When I told the folks I was going, they thought I was crazy. Everyone said I would be killed. I almost think they wished I *would* be killed for being so stubborn. Finally I told Dan, my brother-in-law, to get my team because I had made up my mind. He wouldn't believe me. I told Dan I would as soon be killed by Indians as to live in such a mess as we were living in. When he couldn't change my mind, he decided there was nothing for him to do but to go with me.

We got home about dark. We discovered there were a thousand militiamen, Company E, sent from Omaha and Lincoln to guard our homes, camped a mile or so down the creek. I thought about them in that winter camp. They were probably living on hardtack and water.

The very next morning I built up a good fire and baked bread, cookies, and gingerbread, and I made up a huge batch of doughnuts and sent Dan down to the camp to sell them for me. He sold everything in a couple of minutes. So I baked up more and this time I sent along wild plum jam and chokecherry jelly. Soon I added milk, buttermilk, and eggs to our little business. We discovered we could sell anything to the militiamen at any price we asked. I got quite a bit of Uncle Sam's money—better for them to spend their pay on good food than to gamble or drink it away.

There wasn't any sign of Indians. Although he never said so, I think Dan was glad we had come back to our homes. It turned out it wasn't the Indians we had to worry about. While the people were crowded together in Chadron, the militia kept itself busy by ransacking houses, breaking into the cellars and storage caves. What they didn't eat, they destroyed just for the fun of it. They turned the cattle loose, ran off the horses, and amused themselves by every sort of devilment.

Because Dan and I were on our properties, the militia kept off. I have met people since who have told me, "Oh, I had a brother in that war." "I had a son. He was in the state militia." Nothing to be proud of, if you ask me.

The Indians never made any more trouble. No settler in our area was harmed in any way by an Indian. After about a week Dan drove in to Chadron for Sarah and the children. Some women in the valley didn't come home for ten days, and some for a month, and some went east and never did come back. Ancie was finally allowed to leave Pine Ridge, and we were all glad to be together again. John Shut-the-Door reappeared with his family.

He and Ancie told us some sad stories about what had gone on at Wounded Knee. The soldiers were formed up in three-quarters of a square around the Indian camp, so when they started shooting they hit each other. When boys around them began to fall, the soldiers ran amuck and killed every Indian man, woman, and child that moved. Ancie heard rumors that only one of the soldiers who died was killed by an Indian.

SECTION FIVE
Waking Up

18 ❖ My Companions

Burlington, 1948

When I wasn't listening to stories at home, I sought out children for companionship. I became the friend of two girls of opposite temperament, so unlike each other that it was impossible for the three of us to be together. Lynne, a year younger than I, lived in the house directly opposite ours. Donna Lee, two years older than I, lived in an apartment down around the corner on South Union.

Janus

I could be anything
for anyone. Who was I?
The one who learned
how easy it was
to say yes,
how hard to say no,
who learned to split in two,
knowing all the while
that I was doing it,
one face to this one,
one face to the other.
Who or what was real?

Lynne always wore dresses and never went barefoot. She had blond curls that her mother tied up in cotton strips at night, so they would fall in ringlets around her pretty face. She had big round blue eyes and a little round pink mouth. Lynne and her family attended the same church we did, the First Congregational, but not as often.

In contrast, Donna Lee and I wore shorts all summer and never wore shoes, inside or outside, day or night, except when we were absolutely forced to do so, for church or doctor appointments, for example. Donna Lee had straight brown hair and brown eyes, as did I. Donna Lee's mother had dark skin and darker circles under her eyes and was rumored to be Italian. Donna Lee was Catholic.

Donna Lee and I always played outdoors, while Lynne and I played indoors in her room. In the back of Lynne's closet was a three-drawer dresser in which she kept her sets of paper dolls, hundreds of them. She was allowed a new set every week. Her privilege of ownership meant that only she was allowed to cut out their wardrobes. While she worked her scissors, I lay on her bed reading and rereading her collection of Bobbsey Twins books. Once she had the dolls and their clothes cut out, we played, for the most part without argument, for hours at a time.

The game we played was my idea—orphanage. This allowed us to use many sets of dolls at once. We ignored the differences in their sizes and styles. We grouped them in large imaginary dormitories according to their ages. This was our game. We were their mean and arbitrarily tyrannical overseers. The dolls had to deflect our cruelty to them in the classrooms and dining rooms we pretended into being and ultimately find a way to escape from us.

Lynne was not allowed out after supper to join the wild neighborhood games of statues, kick the can, king of the mountain, or hide-and-seek. After school in the spring and fall, the boys set up a marbles game of their own invention in the driveway of our neighbors up the hill, the Rowells. They dug a shallow hole in the gravel (the Rowells were very easy-going). Each player in turn stood behind a line and tried to toss a marble into the hole. The boys insisted we play "keepsies." By the end of each day's play, the big boys had managed to acquire most of our marbles. However, there was always the chance even a girl might get lucky and win a few of them back.

Lynne had a large collection of beautiful marbles sitting unused in her room. One afternoon I convinced her to bring them outside and join the game. She soon lost several. I was mortified when she began to cry and said she wouldn't play "keepsies" after all. The boys finally relented. She took her marbles back and went home.

Lynne's parents did not eat meals with Lynne and her brother. Her mother served lunch to the two children in the little sun room behind their kitchen. Their lunch was always either a peanut butter or a tuna fish sandwich on brown bread with a dish of fruit cocktail for dessert. I admired that regularity.

My mother was prone to experimentation as a cook, and our lunches were usually leftovers from the night before; beets, reheated, with cold sliced beef heart, or pumpernickel and peanut butter with a side of tomato aspic. We ate all meals together. At lunchtime my brother and I walked home the short two blocks from school and my father the mile down the hill from his office at the university.

Lynne's mother was always kind and welcoming to me. Despite my bare feet, she was happy to have me in to play with Lynne. She did not want Lynne outside with the ruffians.

Donna Lee *was* a ruffian. She was the most adventurous and wild tomboy of all the girls around. With Donna Lee I saw more of the town, met more people, and got in more trouble than in all the rest of my years in Burlington.

She and I met Dr. Morgan when we snuck into his backyard on South Union Street to see pedigreed boxer dogs. Wanting to make friends, we tried to feed them through the wire of their runs with various plants we pulled up from Dr. Morgan's garden. Suddenly Dr. Morgan burst out of his back door to tell us that these were very special dogs on very special diets and WE WERE NOT TO FEED THEM and perhaps we should leave his yard.

I never went back again, but one day Donna Lee told me she had visited many times since and had become a very good friend of Dr. Morgan and his dogs. Such a good friend, in fact, that he had invited her and any friend she wanted to bring to his daughter's wedding reception to be held this very afternoon in his house. I pointed out to Donna Lee that we had been playing hard all day and were pretty dirty. Was she sure we were invited? Was she sure we could go barefoot? Oh yes, she was. So we went.

We walked into a house crowded with grown-ups, the women wearing hats and gloves and beautiful dresses, the men in fancy suits. I thought I saw some of them staring at us, but Donna Lee didn't seem to notice. She walked around until she found a table piled with food and was just starting to load up a plate when a woman approached and told us it was time for us to leave.

I was very embarrassed and was pretty sure that we had not been invited despite Donna Lee's insistence that we had. I was more certain that we should not have come to the party in dirty shorts.

There was usually a suspicion in my mind that whatever I was doing with Donna Lee was probably not the right thing to do. Nevertheless, I went along with most of her suggestions. Clearly I was only her sometime companion, because wherever we went together, she had already been there many times before on her own.

First she took me to visit what must have been most of the horses still stabled in town. She loved horses, and I convinced myself that I did, too. I did love their soft noses and felt sorry for them in their lonely life hidden away in backyards of the city. Visiting them required walking down many new streets, through many yards, and climbing many fences. This in itself was adventure to me who, on my own, had hardly wandered beyond the two blocks encompassing Cliff Street and Adams School. Boys wandered; girls stayed close to home.

Moving away from familiar ground did have risks. In a neighborhood well below South Union Street, in those days a sort of boundary line, we were chased one day by a pack of yelling boys bearing sticks. While looking back over our shoulders at them, we ran full-tilt into an abdomen-high wire stretching across someone's yard. The bad news was that the wire flipped both of us over. We landed sore and breathless on the ground on the other side. The good news was that the boys dissolved into laughing scorn at this sight and decided we weren't worth pursuing.

Next we walked a couple of miles out to the south side of town to visit a riding stable. Donna Lee assured me we could get rides if we helped groom the horses. We hung around for hours while she talked to the stable hands and we brushed the horses, but I never got to ride and I'm not sure Donna Lee did either. When Mother found out where we had been she was horrified. "An eight year-old young lady has no business hanging around riding stables," and I was not to go out there again.

So instead we began to walk the mile and a half up past the university to Centennial Field, where our semi-professional baseball team practiced and played. Donna Lee knew the schedule and managed to get us in to watch practice. Neither of us had money for admission to the actual games, so we stood outside the fence, as close to the dugout as we could, cheering wildly. Donna Lee knew each player by name, and I soon learned the names as well. "Go, Tom!" "Good one, Bill!" I convinced myself that I really did like baseball, although not as much as Donna Lee did, of course. I didn't even know the rules until she explained them to me.

Donna Lee knew something else about the team, the boarding house where the players lived. After practice we would wait for the players on the front steps of their house. Donna Lee wanted to talk to them and get their autographs. The players teased her a lot. I tried to make myself more or less invisible on these occasions out of shyness and the more or less sure knowledge that my mother would not approve of my hanging out there. If no one spoke to me, I wasn't really there. And, in fact, when Mother did find out where we had been going, she put a stop to those expeditions as well.

Our next plan was a moneymaking scheme. We would establish a circus in my back garden. We spent some time assembling costumes from Mother's rag bag and a trunk she let us rifle through in the attic. We set up a ring of bushel baskets and attached a length of clothesline to Gypsy's collar and tried to teach her to clamber up on one basket after another. Always eager for any sort of attention, she was willing, but slow and clumsy. She never did manage to get up on one without it tipping over. Donna Lee thought I might make an acceptable substitute for Gypsy, but even I drew the limit at putting a rope around my neck while Donna Lee wielded a whip.

Then we tried acrobatics, juggling, and a parade, but neither of us proved noticeably adept at the first two, and even we could see that Gypsy and the two of us, no matter how spectacularly garbed we might be, were a pretty poor excuse for the last. It was hard to imagine people paying money to see us.

So we abandoned the circus for something really reprehensible. A girl named Betsy lived in a house down on South Union next to Donna Lee's apartment. I hardly knew Betsy, but since her house and Donna Lee's apartment building were no more than fifteen feet apart, I had often seen Betsy's swing set. Except for Betsy's, the only swing sets I knew about were in public parks. I had also seen her sandbox and her vast array of toys.

Donna Lee pointed out to me that these toys were not well taken care of. They were left out overnight and rusted in the rain. Clearly Betsy did not deserve fine toys. She took such poor care of them. She didn't share her bounty with others certainly more deserving than she. Donna Lee had never once been invited the three or four steps from her back door into Betsy's yard to play. Nor had I, for that matter.

It was essential, Donna Lee insisted, that we teach Betsy a lesson about the necessity for sharing and for taking care of one's unappreciated abundance of *things*. Donna Lee had determined that the swing set could be taken apart easily. The plan was that we remove the pieces one by one and hide them somewhere. Somewhere became the back of my garage under an old quilt we had previously appropriated for the circus.

Over a period of weeks we carried off two swings, a monkey bar, a set of rings, and a seesaw (the latter very tricky, achieved only under the cover of darkness). Finally all that remained of the swing set were the frame and chains dangling empty.

My unease increased daily. What seemed at first only logical and appropriate became to feel mean and very, very naughty. Although Donna Lee insisted we weren't stealing but only instructing, I wasn't so sure. However, once the first ring rested under the quilt, I felt obligated to continue and couldn't think of a way out.

It was with a mixture of terror and sick relief that I answered a knock at the door to discover Betsy's very serious looking father asking to speak to my parents.

My punishment was to carry everything back down the street, to rehang the pieces myself while Betsy and her parents watched me, to apologize, and to promise them I would never steal again. I was officially a bad girl. Overwhelmed by shame and guilt, I knew once and for all I wasn't Jesus.

Although not exactly forbidden to see Donna Lee anymore, my discomfort over this misadventure dissolved our friendship.

My friendship with Lynne had diminished over the course of my busy summer with Donna Lee. It dwindled away to nothing when school began in the fall. Lynne was entering second grade and I was skipped to fourth. The difference in our life circumstances became too great. Besides, her mother had heard that I was worse than a ruffian; I was a thief.

It's useful for a poet
to learn early that she's nothing
special, that she is only
a pair of eyes, a pair of ears.
When she sees the bad girl,
the bad boy, she knows
she is one too or will be
if she isn't very, very careful.
So she watches and listens,
already knowing how sad
the world can be.

19 ❖ Recess

Once upon a time,
before I skipped third grade,
I took things for granted—
the teacher's approval,
reading, math, friends.

Now chain-link encloses
the playground's dirt,
gagging stench of drying weeds.
I stand, back pressed
against the rusty fence,
then scuff slowly along the perimeter,
watch spirals of dust
circle into bleached sky.

Time slogs,
more dispiriting
than the long division
I cannot seem to master.
I wait for the bell,
a stop at the water fountain,
the desperate slow unrolling
of another hot afternoon.

20 ❖ Illness

Burlington, 1944–1952

I don't know if caution in the face of fever was the usual procedure in the pre-antibiotic days of the 1940s, or if my brother's repeated bouts of rheumatic fever had made my mother unusually protective of us. At the first sign of an elevated temperature we were sent to bed. We stayed there until the thermometer registered normal for twenty-four hours and we felt no remaining malaise.

I was jealous of my brother's sickness. When he was ill, my mother read to him at night and after he began to recover tutored him in his schoolwork. Evenings, as long as I appeared to be germ-free, I was permitted into his room to lie on the linoleum floor and listen to the radio—*Sergeant Preston of the Yukon, The Lone Ranger, The Inner Sanctum,* and *Edgar Bergen & Charlie McCarthy.*

As I saw it, illness meant pampering attention, and I was always eager to have some of that for myself. Being ill meant special food brought on a tray, ginger ale while the fever remained high, and then milk toast—never my favorite—and eggnog, which I loved. My mother was usually brisk and preoccupied, but when we were ill, she seemed to slow down a bit and feel sorry for us. "Poor thing," she would say, as she felt my forehead or applied Vicks VapoRub to my throat. At a very early age I learned to stay in bed a little longer than necessary, milking my indisposition for yet another touch.

From books I learned about frail women invalids, sweet-tempered and resigned. Grandmother Wilson seemed to be one of them. I knew she was often "unwell." I could see that my mother felt protective of her and sorry for her. Unfortunately for my future mental health, stimulating those feelings in my mother became a desirable goal.

From my observation, most women appeared to live almost as shut-ins. There were war widows and divorcees who had to work and for whom everyone felt pity. The other women on our street were rarely seen outside their houses during the week except when they shook a rug or a mop. Even Lynne's mother of the flowery cotton wash dress and apron and the soft brown hair, was always in her house. She emerged on weekends when she and the rest of Lynne's family went down to the lake together. Several of the most elderly women appeared so seldom on the street all we knew about them were their names. My grandmother spent most days in her room except Sundays, when she went to church. There were at least two actual recluses on Cliff Street, one of whom was Mrs. Hunt.

My mother, with her committee work, was somewhat of an exception, but I already knew that I could never measure up to Mother. Nor did she seem to wish me to try. I was to behave, do what she told me to do, be a good girl, and not question her decisions.

Being ill, on the other hand, evoked my mother's sympathy.

When I was nine and ten years old, I had a period of actual ill health that, welcome in many ways, had fewer advantages than I expected it should. One drawback was the pain. One day I experienced excruciating and increasing abdominal pain. Mother, according to her usual practice, gave me an enema, despite my insistence that I was not constipated and didn't need an enema. At nine I already knew that enemas were not supposed to be administered for abdominal pain to people who still had their appendixes. I know for sure that I did not dare tell this fact to my mother. I had long since learned that death in silence was easier than opposition to my mother's will. There was no way I could prevent this regular invasion of my body. The enema did nothing to relieve the pain.

The doctor, finally summoned, carried me to his car and drove immediately to the hospital. He performed an emergency appendectomy. Aside from some minor adhesions, he discovered there was nothing wrong with my appendix. My complaints about the continued pain in the following days were met with the doctor's scorn and my mother's embarrassment. Of course I hurt; I had an incision through my abdominal wall.

After a fairly extended period of bed rest, common after surgery in those unenlightened days, I spent weeks bent over in gingerly movement. The doctor, convinced that I was a malingerer with an overactive sense of drama, which, of course, was true, was appalled by my doubled-over posture when I returned for a checkup. He told me I would surely develop more adhesions if I didn't force myself upright. It was time to return to my normal activities. I did, although I continued to be rather draggy and lethargic and to have strong and recurring pain in my abdomen through the fall.

At Christmas we took a family trip to Washington, D.C., to visit my mother's brother and his wife and to see the sights. The pain, fiercer than ever, grew so intense that, unable to stand upright, I climbed the steps of the Lincoln Memorial on my hands and knees. We returned to my uncle's apartment. There, to my utter humiliation, and despite my pleas that I was not constipated, my mother gave me another enema. Of course, it did nothing to diminish the pain. My temperature rose to 106 degrees. Frightened, Mother called a physician.

I was admitted to the Children's Hospital in Washington for five days of inconclusive tests. Released for the long wintry drive home, I lay in the back seat with my head in Mother's lap. In Burlington I entered the Bishop De Goesbriand Hospital for an additional five days. Eventually it was determined that I had a severe kidney infection. I was sent home with one of the newfangled antibiotics, and my parents were told I should have bed rest until I felt better.

For several weeks I did feel quite ill, I think. Kidney infections, I understand, often do cause drastic fluctuations of fever and a sort of overwhelming fatigue, but I know I felt better long before I got up. I was regularly asked how I felt. I would reply that I didn't feel well, not well enough to do any schoolwork. I was much too sick to go back to school. I was filled with dread about both prospects and with guilt about my less than truthful responses.

I did have my meals on a tray. I did have the radio in my room. I spent hours listening to whatever cowboy music I could find and daydreaming about being a cowgirl companion to my beloved Red Ryder or to Gene Autry, my second choice. I thumbed through old *National Geographics*. I was bored, but my dread about getting up was stronger than the boredom of keeping to my bed.

I was alone most of the time. Mother had returned to work by then to serve as executive secretary to the Howard Relief Society, a privately funded welfare organization. Grandmother Wilson stayed mostly in her room. She felt sorry for me. Since she couldn't think what else to do, she brought me snacks—peanut butter and grape jelly on saltines. Although I wasn't the least bit hungry and didn't care for peanut butter and jelly on saltines, I ate them anyway out of politeness and boredom.

Since I was keeper of the radio, evenings sometimes brought me welcome company when Andy would join me to listen to *Lux Radio Theater, Dr. Christian,* and other favorites. For a couple of weeks Mother joined Andy and me for the greatest pleasure of this period of invalidism, the most intense pleasure of my entire childhood. Together, we read Paul Gallico's *The Abandoned.* It is the story of a lonely boy, ignored by his parents, who turns into a cat after being hit by a car. He has many terrifying adventures. The cat who has become like a mother to him dies, and he is at the point of death himself. Some evenings I was overcome by the sadness but, despite the pain I felt for the poor cats, I wanted the story to continue. In the end, the hero doesn't die, but finds himself once again a little boy in the hospital awakening from a coma. In their fear for his life, his parents have come to realize that they do love him after all—just the sort of melodrama I preferred.

We took turns reading aloud. Mother, the former English teacher and debate and drama coach, read with expression, performing the story. My brother, too, read very well. I imitated their methods. My pleasure must have derived from sharing the intense emotions of the story that, I thought, we experienced together. However, the pleasure must have been mostly mine, because we never read together again.

Mother's long experience with my brother's attacks of rheumatic fever had conditioned her to equate illness with stillness, with the need not to exert oneself. Although certainly true for rheumatic fever, it was probably not necessary for the successful treatment of appendectomies, kidney infections, mumps, measles, chicken pox, and all my other childhood ailments. I was grateful for the permission to do less, all the while being quite sure I could do more.

Eventually even I couldn't justify remaining in bed. I got up and returned to school. Thanks to Miss Tinker, my experienced fifth grade teacher, who managed to retain her sense of humor while treating us all with never a hint of favoritism, the rest of the school year was much less unpleasant than I had expected it to be.

It was wonderful not to be the teacher's pet. Miss Tinker reinforced my idea of the advantages of being nothing much, of not being singled out, as I had too often been in my previous years at school.

21 ❖ The Slam Book

Burlington, 1953

A little spiral-bound notebook was slipped surreptitiously into my hand almost every day in seventh grade study hall at Burlington Junior High. My neighbors kept their eyes on me to monitor my handling of this important document, as I kept watch over the girls who had it before me. As the pages of one book filled, another, of equally anonymous provenance, would take its place. It never occurred to me to pass the book along, unread. It never occurred to me to provide a notebook myself.

It was considered bad form to search for the page on which my name had been inscribed in capital letters above the first line. Although both eager and apprehensive to see what was written there, I followed a self-imposed procedure, turning the pages in order. When I did reach my page most of the entries were at least faintly positive—*Ok, Nice, Sweet,* the occasional *Wonderful,* in the recognizable handwriting of my friends Roberta, Beverly or Betsy, and an even more occasional *Ugh.* On the whole, not bad.

Ever since I skipped third grade and found myself achingly isolated and friendless, my number-one goal and greatest ambition had been to become popular. My calculated blandness, my big smile for everyone, seemed to be moving me forward in a generally positive direction.

My own work in these books differed somewhat from my sweetly smiling, compliant, public face. Having only just pulled myself out from the chasm of outcasts, still feeling one unconsidered remark or a moment's careless act away from its edge, I had great sympathy for those who seemed destined never to get out of it. There were the girls who lived out on the North End or, worse yet, on Battery Street, who had front teeth blackened by decay, who wore tight sweaters, who were said to be fast, or who had French-Canadian names. *Patty-the-Pig with the Community Chest.* Or the girls who had good teeth and adequate clothes but who were slow or fat. On their pages filled with words like *Yuck, Ugh, Cheap, P-U, Mean,* or *Nasty,* I would write *Really Sweet* or *Super Nice.* I wasn't a friend to these girls. My only interaction with them was on the pages of the slam books.

There were popular girls who I did not think deserved their position. They had been unkind (to me) or, as far as I could see, lacked any distinction other than of wardrobe or self-confidence. Their pages were filled with *Fantastic, Terrific,* or the hopeful, *My Best Friend.* Beneath their names I would write in carefully disguised penmanship *OK,* or *Stuck-up,* or even, in tiny letters, *Ugh.*

On the pages of the truly worthy, my friends, I would write whatever glowing adjectives were usual in the rather limited vocabulary of the slam. *The Best, Super, A True Friend.* A few girls among those I considered my friends were often *slammed* despite the WASP last names and good grades that should have kept them safely at least in the *OK* category. Perhaps they had bad tempers or didn't keep their hair washed and curled or were too aggressive and successful in class. Under their names I would make several entries, varying my handwriting for each *Fantastic, Really Nice,* or *Great* I sprinkled across their page. I hoped reading the words I wrote would bring a moment's pleasure.

I was aware that whatever I wrote made no real difference. My friends already knew I liked them. My positive words did not enhance their position in the social order. The truly *slammed* girls would not be cheered by a lone entry, especially from someone like me who didn't have the power to change a thing. The generally adored would, probably accurately, consign the negative comment to jealousy.

Whatever comments I wrote were not accompanied by a change in behavior. I did not throw in my lot with the shunned or become less meek or hopeful around the chosen.

By ninth grade the slam books no longer circulated. Perhaps the hierarchy was so firmly established by then that the books no longer served a purpose. Several of the most buffeted girls quit school after the eighth grade for a variety of reasons having nothing to do with the slam books, or at a more fundamental level, everything to do with them. Perhaps the slam book mirrored the general cruelty of their lives. Several of the most honored and lovely departed for boarding schools. The rest of us pretty well knew our places. At the time, those places seemed fixed forever.

> I never could understand
> how someone
> could take pleasure
> hurting another person's feelings,
> especially why the strong
> attacked the weak.
> I hated meanness in myself.
> It was there, of course,
> but I tried to beat it down.
> Although I couldn't see it then,
> the golden ones must have
> had their troubles, too.

22 ❖ Prayer Circle

Burlington, 1954–1957

My second period of religious enthusiasm became a confusing tangle of faith and sex, love, and lust. Until I began high school in 1954, I believed the things I had been taught at the Congregational church. Most of the people I knew seemed to accept the stories. I never put much stock in resurrection, however. I did think that *Jesus* came back to watch over us, but I could not imagine myself nor anyone else I knew as an angel, nor could I believe in a heaven of harps and clouds. I was sure that even my saintly, self-effacing grandmother would never make a sufficient spectacle of herself to appear anywhere in lush white wings.

As a very young child, having lost first my cat and then Granddaddy Nuquist to death and its apparent blank obliteration, death was a bitter, bitter fact. I didn't want to believe in it, but I did. Despite all my frantic desire that they reappear, warm and moving and available to me, both my cat and my grandfather had stayed very decisively dead and buried. When I dared think about it, I knew I, too, would be dead someday.

Solace came for me one day in ninth-grade Latin. We translated from the *Aeneid* the description of Queen Dido's death—"and her life receded into the winds." From that moment I was comforted about my own death. To merge with the matter of the universe was more than sufficient. This became my decidedly unchristian belief.

At about the same time that I rejected this central tenet of Christianity, however, I fell in love with Jesus, at least the Jesus of my own imagination. I heard Harry Belafonte sing, "I think I heard him cry, when they was nailin' in the nails." I felt such pity. For the first time I could participate in the very human agony, and—what seemed to me to be—the injustice, cruelty, and unfairness of His sentence and death.

Of course I had participated all my life in the symbolic reenactments of His life which make up the Christian calendar, from the lighting of the candle on our windowsill each Christmas Eve to welcome Him into the world, to the happy celebration of His entry into Jerusalem on Palm Sunday, to the purple gloom of Good Friday, and ultimately to the lily-scented day of His reappearance. Now, however, Jesus, the unfairly martyred young man, handsome, radically loving and full of understanding, filled my heart. I wanted to become one with His agony. In an excess of devout blasphemy, I came to believe that somehow my passionate faith would soothe His wounds. If I gave my life over to Him, to religion, He would see and be comforted.

So at fourteen, religious practice took up most of my time that was not devoted to school. I attended church every Sunday, sang in two choirs and went to youth group each Sunday evening. I became an officer in a state-wide ecumenical student organization. I felt, even so, more was required of me. Kneeling beside my bed, I prayed each morning and evening. I decided I should become a minister. I had not given full consideration to the limitations of my being female. I had neither realized nor accepted that to become a minister at that moment in history would require a measure of struggle and determination probably always beyond my character.

Eager and able to impose various forms of discipline upon myself, I read the Bible through, a chapter each night, despite understanding very little of what I read. It all seemed a great contradictory muddle. I even forced myself to read every "begat," thinking anything less would be cheating. Jesus was watching and would approve of my effort. It was a relief to stumble upon the occasional story I already knew, Joseph and his brothers' jealousy and betrayal, the friendship of Ruth and Naomi, and, of course, when I finally reached the New Testament, the disparate testimony of the gospels.

For Lent I gave up eating potatoes, desserts, and snacks. Mother tried to weaken or overcome my resolve with repeated offers of cookies, carrots, or a little nibble of this or that. "One little carrot won't hurt." "You need to keep up your strength." "Aren't you hungry after all that exercise?" "What difference does it make whether you eat it now or eat it at dinner?" For once, fortified by self-righteousness, I was able to resist her will.

I didn't swear. I refused to gossip. I smiled at everyone—yea, even unto mine enemies, even unto my mother. As best I could I banished impure thoughts. But whatever I did, it was never enough. More, more was required of me, although I couldn't discover just what was missing.

Then Dr. L. came to First Church as assistant to Dr. J. His title was youth minister, although the implication was clear that when Dr. J. retired, Dr. L. would most likely replace him. The church was large and prosperous at the time, fifteen hundred members, and it still supported the beautiful brick Victorian parsonage where Dr. J. and his wife lived in rather formal splendor. There was a great deal of formality in First Church under Dr. J's leadership. To preach, he wore a morning suit, a cutaway coat with long tails and gray striped trousers, beneath his plain black robe. As he aged, he feared he was failing to reach the young people of the congregation. He did appear remote to most of us.

So Dr. L. was hired and introduced to the congregation one Sunday morning along with his wife and two young children. I was surprised to see such a young man, tall and trim with lots of dark brown hair combed smoothly back from his forehead. Despite his slightly bulging eyes, I thought he was handsome. I was impressed when I heard he had been a very young member of a ski unit during World War II. In Vermont we venerated an expert skier. We were told he was to run the youth groups.

Relaxed and friendly, ever smiling, he brought a lively energy to our youth meetings on Sunday nights. After only a couple of minutes of shyness that first evening, I found him easy to talk with, encouraging and apparently interested in my questions. I began to stay a few minutes at the end of each session to discuss matters of faith and practice. When he suggested a noontime prayer circle to meet once a week in his office, I was all enthusiasm.

During the hour lunch break from school eight or nine of us, including a couple of boys, rushed the half mile to his office in the church on North Winooski Avenue. There while we ate our sandwiches, he talked informally to us about what it meant to be a Christian in a world of temptation and strife. Then we knelt in a circle on the floor and held hands while he led us in prayer. My fervent wish for these sessions was to be next to him so that I might hold his strong but slightly sweaty hand.

From that time on I believe my love for Jesus was muddled together with my lust for Dr. L. Lust, however, that I would have been shocked and horrified to call by its true name. To me it was an overflow of Christian love. Dr. L. could lead me to greater understanding and knowledge of my faith—to purity and self-effacement in the service of Jesus.

In my fervor and need for instruction, I began to visit him in his office after school several afternoons a week. At the end of our discussions he often drove me home in his green Chevrolet, "since it is a long walk for you and not out of my way." At the curb in front of my house, he would hold my trembling hand as we prayed together.

Had I dared be honest with myself, I would have wondered at my rapid breathing. Could my flustered rapture, my panting adoration, all be explained by an excess of faith? I knew I loved him but was sure it was a pure Christian love—wasn't he, after all, the human representative, the messenger of Jesus?

The next fall at a dance I met Dick, a young man from Montpelier. He liked me. I decided to like him. Soon, very soon, I wore his ring on a chain around my neck. The ring granted Dick permission to find a secluded place to park off Cliff Street after our weekly date. I was no longer separate from but immersed in a world of temptation, about which I felt considerable guilt. I began to feel uncomfortable, even squeamish, in Dr. L's company. I stopped visiting his office and avoided being alone with him. Soon I was too busy at school to find time for prayer circle.

Being certain that I was required to choose either the excitement of Saturday nights in the big black Pontiac or faithfulness to Dr. L. / Jesus, I couldn't relinquish the former for the latter. Faith dissolved in lust and shame, never, I'm sorry to tell, to be regained.

From time to time, however, usually while singing, a sort of religious ecstasy has come over me. In those moments it has seemed to me that I could feel myself disappear, my life already merged with the one vast wind.

And then too, when I die, I hope my family will remember to play Marian Anderson singing "Erbarme dich, mein Gott" ("Have Mercy on Me, My God") from Bach's *St. Matthew Passion*. It is the aria that follows Peter's third denial of ever having known Jesus.

SECTION SIX

A Little Independence

23 ❖ The Driver

1950–1957

It always must be heard. There isn't any other tale to tell, it's the only light we've got in all this darkness.

—James Baldwin, *Sonny's Blues*

As soon as I learned to read, I disappeared from the tidiness of our house into stories with all their complicated emotions that were otherwise not permitted through the door. With my legs over one arm of the brown plush chair in the living room and my head propped against the other, I learned about shipwrecks, pioneers, brocaded palaces, adultery, and murder.

My mother never censored my reading. As a child who loved to read, she often had books taken from her hands by Granddaddy Wilson. He replaced them with the Bible, the only book he considered necessary for her. Consequently, I was permitted to read straight through our shelves, from Bess Streeter Aldrich to Balzac, Cather to Dickens, de Maupassant to Hugo. I believed every word I read, but I thought the hate, violence, and terrible passions were aberrations from regular life, the quiet rational life I knew first-hand.

In our house punishment followed misdeed with unvarying firmness. Everything was done, we were assured, for our own good. I still made mistakes and did bad things, but I was led to believe that I would know better by the time I grew up. I would take my place in the good American world.

Evil was something that could be conquered as we had conquered Hitler, that foreign devil, who did not understand about the clean white-painted pews of the First Congregational Church and liberty and justice for all.

In 1953 during seventh grade I worked in the library. My duties consisted of stamping the due date in the back of an occasional book.

The library was not a busy place. Instead of using my time to do homework, I read books, again selected from the shelves more or less at random.

One day I discovered a memoir written by a black man named Will Thomas. The book was entitled *The Seeking*. The pages seethed with anger and skepticism that the wall of prejudice he had encountered could ever be climbed. Mr. Thomas wrote about his own shocked discovery, in early adolescence, of Jim Crow laws, separate toilets, bad schools, lynchings, and random beatings. Mr. Thomas's life seemed a continual punishment for something for which he was not responsible—his color. I was stunned! It wasn't fair!

Unlike the fiction I never questioned, I was skeptical that this memoir could be true. In the United States of America? I asked my father about it, hoping he would tell me it couldn't. When he said the story certainly could be and most likely was true, I was frightened.

By the end of the book, after planning to move his family to Haiti to find a life free of racial prejudice, he made an almost quixotic decision to move to Vermont, the first state, in 1791, to outlaw slavery. In Vermont he had found space to live and friendly, if taciturn, neighbors. I was glad that there was someplace where he could make a home. I didn't want him to be an angry wanderer forever. Proud that Vermont seemed to be the place, I was so relieved the story had a happy ending.

Most of the villages surrounding Burlington were too small to support junior high and high schools. Many children, after completing sixth grade in a village school, were bused into town. One of my seventh-grade classmates was a black girl named Anne Smith, although she wasn't black at all, rather a pale soft brown. As we became acquainted, I discovered Anne lived in the same village where Mr. Thomas had settled. I asked her if she knew him. She was his daughter!

Anne was the first relative of a real author I had ever known. Excited, I told her that I had read her father's book. Then I remembered what the book said about the closed doors in his life and how often he stood before them, filled with hate and despair. I was suddenly embarrassed to say anything more.

In my own mind, at least, *The Seeking* was both a bridge and a wedge between Anne and me. I never dared talk to Anne about the things the book had taught me. I was afraid Mr. Thomas's story was partly hers. It seemed I knew Anne's secrets, things I shouldn't know. For the whole year it was always the three of us, Anne and me and her father, even though I never met him. I would have been tongue-tied in awe had the opportunity arisen.

The next fall she was gone. I never knew where she went or if Mr. Thomas's search had not ended in Vermont after all. I didn't hear of him or Anne again, but the world was never the same for me after reading his book.

My ninth-grade civics teacher, Mr. Carter, looked like the Devil. His face was covered with bright red freckles, and he had a sharply pointed chin and pointed ears beneath thinning sandy hair. He wore the world's ugliest ties—great wide garishly hand-painted things of burgundy or orange.

When we were particularly careless or stupid, Mr. Carter would grab the long pole that hooked and unhooked the old-fashioned windows and stomp up and down the aisles, raging, banging the pole into the floor, threatening to bash us with it or to throw us out the windows. Although fairly confident he wouldn't really hit us, we were unsettled by these outbursts.

But we maintained a conspiracy of silence. No one ever told on him because in between tantrums he was a wonderful teacher. We knew he was exhausted all the time. The father of eight children, he worked nights as a short-order cook so he could afford to teach us during the day.

Mr. Carter loved the Constitution and the Bill of Rights. He loved the fact that he could vote and that we, too, would have that privilege some day. He insisted we love those things as well. He cajoled and bullied us to attention. We felt very protective towards him.

One day, with great pride and his usual passion, he brought some of his collection of jazz, blues, and folk records to class and tried to help us hear what this music was all about. I had never heard any of it before. When Odetta's rich voice sang "Southern trees bear strange fruit ... blood on the leaves ... blood at the root ... scent of magnolia, sweet and fresh ... sudden smell of burning flesh," the contrast between her beautiful voice and the terrible words froze me.

The broken bodies hung there before my eyes. The world irrevocably tilted another fraction.

In 1957 when I was sixteen, I was chosen to participate in a summer exchange program sponsored by the American Field Service. My role was to go to Luxembourg as a representative American youth to learn from my host family as much about their country as I could. Vastly excited, I was caught up in the adventure and the honor of having been selected to tell about America.

My host parents, Monsieur and Madame Biwer, and Solange, their nineteen-year-old daughter, and Mr. Biwer's elderly father, also a member of their household, picked me up at the train station in Luxembourg City. After we shook hands all around, they told me they liked to assist young people whenever they could. They had housed a French orphan when she didn't have any other place to go. They had sheltered a young refugee from Yugoslavia. Within the first minutes of our acquaintance, I was reduced from proud junior ambassador to humble seeker of refuge. The rest of the summer was equally unsettling.

Luxembourg Summer, 1957

Sixteen years old,
finding myself
in someone else's
reality, absorbed
in details, the first and
fortunate step away
from my mostly
comfortable childhood.

Everything a revelation—
matters small—cheese and ham
for breakfast, passion
in the preparation of food,
selection of wine—
and large—what it meant
to have been hungry,
silenced, surrounded
by death, to hate your
neighbor, to never forgive,

to be formal in every
human interaction, to be
as bound by rules
as I had been at home,
but by different rules.
For the first time
I considered relativity,
took a tiny step towards
a questioning mind.

The Biwers, sure that memories of past wars and fear of future wars dominated my life as it did theirs, wanted to give me the opportunity to honor the American dead, for whom they felt such concern and gratitude. I had given very little thought to the American dead. I worked up a polite interest in the trip to the military cemetery where General Patton is buried, at Hamm, outside Luxembourg City. The trip was planned for the first Sunday of my stay.

The five of us crowded into the Biwers' old Vedette for the drive to Hamm. The Biwers explained to me that as the war was ending, when the grave markers were only rough boards nailed together and hung with dog tags, the people of Luxembourg felt bad that the American boys lay alone, so far from home. People began to visit the cemetery, adopting a few graves, bringing flowers to them, as though they marked the resting places of their own sons. As Monsieur Biwer parked the car, he told me they were glad my visit had caused them to make this trip again.

I soon stood in dismay among those endless, endless rows of white marble crosses and stars of David that marked the remains of the young men who died in 1945 in the frozen forests of the Ardennes. There in the cemetery, Monsieur Biwer asked me a question. "Why in America do white people hate Negroes?"

Shocked speechless, I was desperately embarrassed. I remembered I was a goodwill ambassador, but I was also full of the short course provided by Mr. Thomas and Mr. Carter. I fumbled for words. I tried to assure them that, although true in some parts of the country, Vermont must be different, and I certainly didn't and....

Impatient, Monsieur Biwer interrupted me to tell this story. In 1944 a column of General Patton's Third Army crossed the French border into Luxembourg. Esch-sur-Alzette was one of the first towns they came to, and the Biwer home stood on the main north-south road. All day the column of liberators rolled by.

The Biwers leaned out their second-story windows to wave blankets or towels, or whatever came to hand, in joy and appreciation of the men riding by on tanks and trucks. They ran down to their garden to throw flowers and kisses to the soldiers riding in troop transports or marching by on foot. Church bells rang out. People cheered and wept. The soldiers tossed gum, oranges, chocolates, even a box of Band-Aids to little Solange where she sat on the garden wall with her mother. In her short and hungry wartime life, these gifts were all something she had never seen before.

When the column stopped to rest, Monsieur Biwer went out the gate to the troop transport parked in front and invited the soldiers in it to please come in, sit at their table, and share whatever food there was. They had fixed everything for them. They would be honored.

So the men came and crowded the dining room, poking each other, noisy and cheerful. The Biwers were delighted by these funny boys, these strange loud Americans, at this wonderful moment of deliverance from the Nazis.

But Madame Biwer looked out the window and noticed that the driver had not come in with the other men. This wouldn't do. They must *all* share in this happiness; everyone must eat. So this time Madame Biwer went out to the truck. "Come, Come you must eat. We have prepared enough for all. Do us this honor. Please, please come in."

"Thank you, ma'am, but I'm not hungry—I better stay here. Thank you kindly but I already ate."

The soldier declined politely every way he could, but Madame Biwer continued to insist. Finally Monsieur Biwer joined her, and they half-pulled the soldier from the truck. They pulled him through the gate and up the walk, laughing at his reluctance. They assured him he should not worry, there was still some wine for him, and they entered the dining room.

There was sudden stone silence. None of the men seated around the table greeted him or spoke at all. All the forks, bottles, and glasses were held absolutely still. The Biwers tried to make a place for him at the table. No man would move his chair. The driver yanked his arms free. With a groan, he ran from the room.

The Biwers were stunned to see a man so shamed. The men in the dining room appeared to forget the interruption, ate, drank, and joked just as before. The Biwers gradually poured themselves back into grateful hospitality, but as the soldiers straggled back to the truck, Monsieur Biwer beckoned one of them aside. He had to understand what had happened in his house, to know the meaning of what had been done at his table.

If the soldier would please tell him—his English was not so good. Perhaps there was something he had not understood. Was the driver a bad man? A collaborator with the Nazis perhaps? He had done something terrible, no?

"Oh no, nothing like that," the soldier told him casually, "but in America, Niggers know better than to try to eat at a white man's table."

The driver haunts my life.

24 ❖ Flirting

AFS Summer, 1957

The parting from my parents was easy, but I cried when Dick kissed me and said good-bye. My parents invited him to accompany us to the pier in Montreal in June of 1957. There, along with hundreds of other American Field Service students, I boarded the *Arosa Kulm* for its eleven-day voyage to Rotterdam.

The *Arosa Kulm* was built in 1912 as a freighter. During World War II she had been converted to ferry troops. Now leased by the American Field Service for a few voyages each summer, she flew a Panamanian flag and operated with a German crew.

My cabin was located at the prow of the ship, in D Deck, down three sets of steep ladders. Six girls shared three bunk beds in a space about half the size of my bedroom at home. There was no storage place. We piled our suitcases one on top of the other just to the left of the door. To the right of the door was a tiny sink. The communal showers and toilets were across the gangway from our cabin.

We were two decks below water level. When the lights were turned off, the cabin was in total darkness, the most profound darkness I had ever experienced. Once we were underway, each day a sailor knocked politely at our door. When we let him in, he opened a steel door in our floor. He let down a device to measure the depth of water in the bilge that we could hear sloshing below us.

By the first evening it was clear none of us would spend time in our cabin except to sleep. Right away I became chummy with Jane, a cabin mate on her way to England. We went to dinner together where we stared at gray meat and watery boiled potatoes. The creamed spinach was the exact texture and color of the freshly applied deck paint, thick and still wet in corners.

After dinner we made our way to the crowded lounge. There we squeezed onto a sofa with some laughing boys she had met that afternoon in an introductory meeting. They were also on their way to England. The funniest and friendliest of all was Greg, tall and lean, with gaunt and vaguely Lincolnesque features.

After that first evening, I began to seek out Greg and his group at every opportunity. While Dick was as intense, ambitious, serious, and socially awkward as I, Greg was off-hand and funny. It took two days to sail down the St. Lawrence to the Atlantic. I spent them laughing and flirting outrageously with Greg in a manner entirely new to me. Dick was relegated to the status of guilty secret.

One flirtatious afternoon as we lay around on deck, lounging on the rubber life rafts, one of the boys said to me he was sure I would be married by the time I was nineteen. I knew he meant it as a nasty crack about my behavior toward Greg, but I was flattered in spite of myself.

I had feared boys would never like me. There were the problems of my height, big feet, glasses, and the dowdy clothes my mother made for me. There were my good grades and my eagerness to give the answers in class even if a boy had his hand up, too. Then I played hard in gym class and enjoyed pushing my body and working up a sweat.

Dick had seemed attracted to me despite my disqualifying flaws. When he asked me to be his steady, I thought I had better accept. I was already fourteen. It might be my only chance. There were many good reasons to say yes.

He liked me. Since he wanted me to be his steady, it was even possible he thought I was pretty. He was six feet three inches tall, so I didn't have to worry about my height when I was with him. He had a beautiful bass voice and played piano enthusiastically by ear. He got good grades, even better than mine. He too liked sports, but, like me, he wasn't especially talented at them. He sat on the bench for his basketball team. He could do jumps and spins on his size-twelve figure skates.

Best of all, he lived forty miles away in Montpelier. All week long I could be as competitive as I liked in class. I could even secretly compete with Dick. I didn't have to worry about what I did or said or wore, and still I could be sure of a date for the big dances or parties.

Very soon, too, I discovered I liked the sensations that arose in me while we necked and petted in his black Pontiac. He would very much have liked to "go all the way," and I was always tempted, but since I was definitely not a "fast" girl, it didn't happen.

And now, so quickly, Dick was more or less forgotten.

The ship took a northerly route across the ocean, past icebergs and through very rough seas. Many people were seasick, some for days at a time. The cabins without portholes were dark, airless, and full of vomiting teenagers. I spent much of my day outside on the crowded top deck, no matter how cold, wet, or windy the weather.

Although I often felt queasy, I was never actually sick. I even went to every meal and confronted the unvarying gray meat, watery boiled potatoes, and vegetable creamed to mush. I lost ten pounds in the course of the voyage.

Often we were expected to go to the lounge or the dining room for meetings with the other students going to our particular country, for language classes, or for some other group activity. I signed up to sing in the chorus that practiced inside, but as soon as a meeting or a practice was over, I headed back out to the deck.

The gang going to England hung out there, too. The group was so bright and entertaining and Greg so very attractive that I wasn't eager for the journey to end. I discovered, as well, that I loved the smack and slide of the ship down one wave and then up the next, the cold spray across the deck, and the endless horizon all around us. I was titillated by my freedom and its accompanying sense of danger.

As the ship was about to enter Rotterdam harbor, Greg and I spent the entire last night on deck. He sat leaning against an air vent, and I sat between his legs, my head resting against his chest, his arms around me. We were sealed in a pearly bubble of fog. The bells rang steadily. We could sense ships passing just a few feet from us by a disturbance in the air and the vibration of our ship, and, of course, by the ringing of their bells. Much of the time we sat in companionable silence.

We were both excited about the coming summer and wondered aloud about what might happen. I knew he had a girlfriend back in Michigan, and he knew about Dick. I was quite sure I didn't care any more about Dick. I was afraid Greg considered me a passing and guilt-provoking fancy, a fickle temptress. As the rising sun turned the fog to shimmering blue, we said good-bye. Greg hugged me and was gone. All summer I hoped for a letter. It never arrived.

Once in Luxembourg I didn't pine for long. A week or so after I came to live with the Biwers, a party was arranged in Differdange for the nine of us who had come for the summer and for as many "returnees" as could be rounded up. Returnees were the young Luxembourgers who had spent a year at school in the United States. The Biwers informed me that they had met some of the returnees and had not been impressed by their manners. They had become terribly lax and informal. I should be careful and not be too friendly with any of them, particularly with any of the young men.

At the party, I soon became aware that I was the object of what even I had to admit were admiring glances from a wavy-haired boy standing with John, one of my fellow Americans. John brought him over to be introduced to the Biwers and to me. His name was Armand and he had spent a year in Ohio. Very properly he bowed and shook hands all around before asking the Biwers if he might dance with me. Satisfied that he was still correct in his manners, they said he might.

The party was in the home of John's host family. A space for dancing had been cleared in their elegant salon, the carpet rolled, the furniture moved to the perimeter of the room where the adults, our chaperones, sat. Music came from a phonograph playing slow, slightly old-fashioned American pop songs. In Luxembourg, Bing Crosby, Perry Como, and Frank Sinatra had not yet given way to rock and roll.

Armand and I took our place in the center of the floor. Armand asked me to call him "Mickey." It had been his nickname in America, but no one in Luxembourg would call him anything but Armand.

Mickey was easy to talk to and easy to dance with. He led very well and soon pulled me close, my cheek nestled against his. He didn't seem to mind that I was as tall as he was. We danced together as much as his sense of propriety would allow. I wasn't used to being so obviously admired. I was as reluctant as he to say good night when it was time to shake hands all around once again in a formal Luxembourg farewell. I hoped I would see Mickey soon.

There weren't, however, many opportunities to get together. He didn't live in Esch. Young people didn't have access to cars. Young men did not pay visits or telephone young women, so we had to wait for a party in order to see each other. There were only three more over the summer.

At the first of these events, John took me aside to tell me Mickey had made sure to be included so he could spend the evening with me. The attraction was certainly mutual, and I was flattered by his attention. I did worry a little. Was there something wrong with him, something a little strange and weak that made him find *me* so appealing? Couldn't he do better? Nevertheless, I enjoyed his company.

For the final three days of our stay, all nine of us and many returnees were put up in homes in Luxembourg City so that we might see the sights together. Mickey and I, as part of the larger group, enjoyed the excursions.

There was a culminating evening banquet at one of the downtown hotels, preceded by a reception. Chatting with Mickey and the rest of our by now close-knit group, I happened to look up in time to see the entrance of a young god, the most handsome boy I had ever seen. He was tall, slender, broad-shouldered, with a classical profile and curly black hair, elegantly attired in a perfectly fitted sports coat and tie. The sort of boy I instinctively avoided, he was too beautiful ever to notice me except with disdain. I couldn't keep myself from admiring him, however—inconspicuously, I hoped—always careful to look away and avoid meeting his eyes.

When we took our places at the table, this god was seated on my left! We introduced ourselves, and it was almost immediately apparent to me that Pascal was less sure of himself and I much more poised than I had thought possible. Pascal was from a very strict and formal Catholic family. He was an only child and attended a boys' school. I don't believe he had ever had a relaxed and open conversation with a girl before. I was a foreigner, a Protestant, an American girl traveling without my family. To him such a girl was enchantingly easy and approachable.

He told me everything about himself. He was soon to attend university to study international law like his father and grandfather before him. His father was a lawyer for the European Coal and Steel Community. Pascal was a member of the American Field Service Club and had very much hoped to spend a year in America, but his parents wouldn't permit it. They did not approve of the things they heard about American teenagers. They did not want him to lose a year of school. They knew American schools were less rigorous than schools in Luxembourg.

He wanted to know all about my life in America and seemed delighted by every little thing I told him. By now I had found much to admire in Luxembourg and could see much that was lacking in America. At home I had always considered myself somewhat of an outsider, but in me Pascal saw all he had imagined about American teenage life. I admired his erudition, sophistication, the perfect cut of his black hair, and the green and burgundy checks in his elegant silk sports coat. For the next three hours we talked together, ignoring everyone else.

Mickey was seated several places away from me on the other side of the table. I pretended not to notice his resentful glances.

When the banquet was over, much too soon to suit either Pascal or me, the whole group was scheduled to continue on to an amusement park as our final entertainment. Outdoors, Pascal and I were directed into separate taxis. Reunited at the park, Pascal had time only to write my address on a little slip of paper. He was already late. He had to be home by midnight, he told me, and, like Cinderella, he fled.

Mickey avoided me for the rest of the evening.

The next day we were back on the train to Rotterdam and reboarded the *Arosa Kulm*. Greg made it immediately clear that our flirtation was over. The eleven-day trip home was enjoyable even without the added *frisson* of flirtation.

I knew Dick was coming with my parents to meet me at the dock. I dreaded seeing him. All summer I had treated him more than shabbily. Not only had I flirted with every boy who came my way, I had stopped writing letters to Dick by my second week in Luxembourg. I had taken the chain holding his ring off my neck and put it in the bottom of my suitcase. But I had neglected to tell him I didn't want to be his steady anymore. I had left him to worry and wait for my return.

But Dick was not to be deterred. He persisted, despite my turning aside his kiss, despite my sliding away from him to the opposite side of the back seat for the long drive home, despite my telling him, finally, when we were alone in the backyard in Burlington that I didn't think we should go steady any more. He continued to write me, to call, to ask me for dates.

Finally he wore me down. I agreed to keep the ring. Officially, while he was away for his first year in college, I was his somewhat reluctant steady during my senior year in high school. Soon after the ring was back on my neck, I received a long and friendly letter from Pascal. I didn't answer it.

By the time I began college, I decided I did love Dick after all and told him so. This surrender is what Dick had been waiting for. A month or two into my freshman year, he unceremoniously dumped me. I was hurt and angry, but somewhere in the back of my mind, I had to admit it was about what I deserved.

> Jezebel,
>
> but wasn't she beautiful,
> full of disdain?
>
> While I forget the one before,
> desire the new, I go only so far.
>
> I hold on to that last
> little speck of flesh.
>
> I imagine she gave her body
> away while keeping herself
> to herself.

25 ❖ Remembrance Day

Ettelbruck, Luxembourg, July 1957

The Biwers were excited as we drove to Ettelbruck. We were going to the third annual celebration of Remembrance Day, honoring the memory of General George S. Patton and the American Third Army. Heroes, they reminded me. German troops occupied Ettelbruck on May 10, 1940. A memorial was erected at the exact spot where Patton and his army halted the Germans on Christmas Day 1944, during the Battle of the Bulge. The liberation was still fresh, a joyous memory. Even Grandpa smiled. Solange, as always, was quiet.

We managed to find a place to park and worked our way through the crowds to the monument, passing buses filled with American soldiers waiting to assemble for the parade. I was a little embarrassed but secretly happy and flattered by the whistles and comments directed my way. It was great to hear English, even rude English, probably ruder than if they had known I could understand what they were saying. I was glad I was wearing my prettiest dress, a narrow waist, full skirt, black-and-brown polished cotton, a deep V neckline in the front and back. I wished they would whistle at Solange. I couldn't understand why they didn't. After all, I was the one with glasses.

Everyone seemed happy this day. There were smiles on every face, loud applause for Patton's son, also a military man, and for his young grandchildren. They took their places on a platform set up in front of the memorial. Even the rain had stopped for the family of the grand duchess and various civilian and military dignitaries to give their salutes and greetings and speeches. We all cheered as soldiers marched by through streets where terrible fighting had taken place thirteen years before. I was so proud to be an American.

After the last speech and anthem and final salute, we joined the crowd that headed toward the enormous tent the American army had provided. Inside, the five of us occupied a table from where we had a good view of the temporary bandstand and dance floor. Soon it filled—tables of soldiers, tables of Luxembourgers. The tent smelled of beer and frying sausages.

At the table next to us were eight black soldiers. One of them, I had not failed to notice, was extremely handsome, tall and fit and a lovely shade of caramel—nor had he failed to notice me. The band played, soldiers began to ask girls to dance, and soon the soldier politely asked me, or indicated by pantomime, if I would like to dance. Monsieur Biwer gave his smiling assent.

My soldier led me to the floor. Glad to be able to speak English, to understand and be understood, I told him I was an American. He stiffened.

"So? So? What difference does that make?"

I said I was so glad to hear English.

He still seemed a little put out. I was afraid he thought I mentioned being an American because I was white and he was black, or maybe it was only because I was aware of that, and trying not to be that made me oversensitive. I wasn't sure he believed me.

I've never been a good dancer—too self-conscious. At this moment I was even more awkward from embarrassment, but we stayed together for several numbers—long enough to make small talk, to learn his name, now forgotten, and he mine, long forgotten, too, I'm sure, to learn that he was from Chicago, and to tell him I was from Vermont, that he was twenty-six and I was sixteen, that he was stationed in Germany, and I was spending the summer in Luxembourg, and for him to ask if I would like to step out for some fresh air. Oh, I wanted to. I was both regretful and relieved to tell him I didn't think the Biwers would like that. He led me back to the table.

There was a pause. Glances were directed my way from the adjoining table. I could tell he and his friends were talking about me. Then one by one those soldiers invited me to dance. I had somewhat regained my poise and was able to make polite conversation with each new partner. I realized Mr. Handsome and I had become accomplices, coconspirators in a racial experiment in which I was a knowing participant.

The soldiers asked me in strict order, first those from the north, then from the south and handsome, then from the south, not handsome, and finally a sweaty-palmed, overweight, trembling young man from Alabama who could barely say a word. I was too young and shy myself to be of much help—one polite dance each.

And then that was that. Monsieur and Grandpa collected their beer and sausages, brought us our *limonade*. No one invited Solange. I couldn't tell if it bothered her or if she was relieved. I minded for her.

The soldiers sat at their table and we sat at ours until a very young white soldier asked me to dance. I told him he must ask Monsieur Biwer, who gave his permission. We danced a few dances; he was also from Alabama. Nice enough. When he walked me back, he casually sat down uninvited at our table. Why did he assume he had the right? What would Monsieur Biwer think? Why had I not asked Monsieur Biwer if *my* soldiers could move over? What must *they* have thought?

I wished I were from Luxembourg, or France, or any of the places I was sure were more civilized than the U.S.A. When we rose to leave, the white soldier asked for my address. I pretended not to hear.

26 ❖ Lying

Vassar College, 1959

May 1959, the end of my freshman year at Vassar. One of the best things about college was the freedom to lie to my family that distance provided. I became an expert.

Lying was relatively easy most of the year, because my parents were away in Beirut, Lebanon. My father had a one-year Smith-Mundt appointment to teach American government at American University. Before the year was over, however, my Grandmother Wilson had unexpected surgery. Mother returned to Burlington early to be with her.

So Mother was back in Vermont. Two weeks before school closed, I discovered that, due to sloppy management of my first checkbook, I had at my disposal not twenty-five dollars but twenty-five cents. All year I had enjoyed writing checks, but I found entering them in the check register to be very tedious.

My parents had only reluctantly given me permission to attend Vassar.

"You know, Elizabeth, it's not as though we have extra money to throw around. I don't understand why the University of Vermont is not good enough for you. It would cost us practically nothing. You would get free tuition and you could live at home. You could get a perfectly adequate education right here. Don't you think you might be hurting your father's feelings? You don't think he has been a good teacher to his students?"

I thought, indeed, I might be hurting my father's feelings, but I persisted. Eventually my parents agreed to pay $1,100 a year, the difference between the $2,500 cost of annual tuition and board and my $1,400 scholarship, but only if and as long as I could pay all my own expenses. I was told to consider the first year an experiment subject to that condition. I had earned enough at my summer job as a waitress at a local restaurant that I was confident I'd have enough money for the school year.

But now it would cost at least twenty dollars in train and bus fares to make the trip home from Poughkeepsie to Burlington. If I revealed my stupidity to my parents by asking for money, I wouldn't be permitted to return for my sophomore year. What could I do? The days when girls hitchhiked from place to place alone were still in the future; I never considered such an option.

For my own self-respect and despite my frequent terror of the place, I was desperate to continue at Vassar. The scholarship director, young, attractive, immaculately suited and quietly sadistic, called me often to her office for stern admonitory lectures. She reminded me that there were many deserving applicants who could use my scholarship money if I couldn't keep my grades up. Was I sufficiently applying myself to my studies? Did I feel capable of maintaining the necessary requirements? Trying to project a certainty I didn't feel, I lied that I was sure my grades would all be above a B. I worried that most everyone I had met, professors and fellow students alike, suspected I was not Vassar material. I didn't want to prove any of them correct.

In a panic I wrote Andy, who was finishing his senior year at Wittenberg University in Ohio. He had the use of the family car for the semester, since no one anticipated Mother's early return.

Begging for secrecy, I asked if he would drive out of his way to pick me up. Would he please pretend it was his idea? He responded that he would be glad to come for me but, as I already knew, there was a three-day discrepancy in the closing dates of our respective schools. He would not be able to arrive until three days after the Vassar campus closed. I answered that I didn't care. I would wait for him. He was saving my life.

These were the luxuriously intimate days when almost all of Vassar's fourteen hundred students were required to live in dormitories. Each dormitory had its own dining room. At the final breakfast in Raymond House, there was a big bowl of oranges on the serving counter. I took the one permitted me back to my table and lingered there, jumping up when one of my friends entered the cafeteria line.

"Are you going to eat an orange this morning? No? Well, will you take one for me then, please?" By the end of the meal, I had nine oranges stashed away in my bag. After breakfast, I dropped fifteen cents into the snack machine for a package of peanut butter cheese crackers. I saved my last dime so that I would be able to make a telephone call if some emergency forced me to confess my situation.

Mary Rockefeller lived in rather grand isolation on my corridor that year. Although I rarely saw her, I heard rumors that a decorator had come in to do her room and that she went to a hairdresser for a weekly wash and set. She passed us, poor and lowly freshmen, without a glance. I don't remember her ever being in the communal lavatory brushing her teeth at the sink, but perhaps we knew enough to avert our eyes. Before she departed, she tossed all the paperbacks she had purchased for her courses into a big heap in the hallway next to the trash. I gleaned the pile and now possessed *Clarissa* with *Mary Rockefeller* written dauntingly on the first page.

I spent my next few days reading the book, slipping around the empty campus, but never staying in one place for more than an hour. Fortunately the weather was fine—sunny, although a bit cool. I sat on the bank of Vassar Lake, moving on at the noise of an approaching lawn mower. I skulked to a bench beneath fading azaleas in Shakespeare Garden, disappearing through the hedge when voices sounded nearby. Hidden in the shadow of one of the big trees on the library lawn, I kept my head down over my book, hoping not to be recognized or questioned.

Careful to ration my food, I permitted myself one peanut butter cheese cracker and an orange per meal for the first two days. The third day, my meal at breakfast, lunch and supper was merely an orange.

At night I waited until the woman at the desk, the "white angel," as such employees were bizarrely called, went to dinner or on break. "Angels" were required to wear white uniforms that marked them as both figures of authority and of diminished social status. There was a member of the administration known as the warden in those days of *in loco parentis,* and the angels worked for her as guardians of the door and of the curfew and for us as our message takers. It became apparent that, at least for the first few days school was not in session, the angels remained on duty.

I lurked in the shadows until the angel left her post and then crept up to my old room, now stripped of everything including sheets and blankets. Stretched out on the bare mattress in my clothes, I slept fitfully, aware that the dorm was completely empty except for me and the night watchman making his rounds. I kept my door closed. None of the doors had locks.

I didn't turn on a light but got up as soon as there was sufficient daylight to see, washed quickly in the cavernous bathroom at the end of the hall, and tried to be as inconspicuous as possible sneaking downstairs and out the door. The night watchman surely knew I had been there, and the angel knew too, but neither challenged my presence. My luggage remained in a heap by the front door, carried down as instructed after the last breakfast. Technically, therefore, I had met the regulations by moving out of my room. The staff was used to the strange and inexplicable behavior of students.

The first day I had said something vague to the angel about waiting for my brother who had been unexpectedly delayed, so I was prepared when she caught me slipping out the door the third morning. In answer to her inquiry, I assured her there was absolutely no doubt that my brother was coming for me; in fact he would probably arrive within the hour.

Fortunately, I had practiced lying all year, not only to my parents, but to the angels as well. For example, I hadn't really been at the Vassar Club in Manhattan; instead, I stayed in the grubby Greenwich Village apartment of some boys who had recently graduated from Hamilton College. It became routine to provide, as necessary, false information about where I might be found. I grew more confident with each undetected fabrication.

This time, however, I was in terror of discovery. College friends who have since heard of my predicament asked why in heaven's name I hadn't told them about it. They would have taken me home or lent me money. The former was no solution at all, because it would have still left me with no means of getting from their home to my home. For the latter I was too ashamed and too proud to reveal myself as being so poor and helpless. I would rather pass out on the street, starving, my hair falling out in handfuls around me, like the hero of Knut Hamsun's *Hunger,* one of my favorite novels at the time. Hunger was preferable to the humiliation of admitting my need, but I did feel a fool for not keeping track of my funds.

Mother considered it a moral lapse to seek favors, advice, or scholastic help. One was to make one's way in the world on one's own merit. Asking for help was on a par with the disgrace of sex before marriage—both were unthinkable.

Then, too, I didn't want to expose my mother to criticism from my hallmates or reveal to them once again my fear of her. Early in the year, before she left for Lebanon, she had telephoned me. Called to the hall phone, I knew the news must be dire. Mother was of the generation that believed long-distance calls were reserved for emergencies only, too extravagant for general use. It was the only time she telephoned in four years.

She announced that, judging from my letters, I was having too much fun on weekends. She and my father were convinced I was not being serious enough about my studies. Therefore, for the four years I was at Vassar, I was not to date.

If I wanted to go to such an expensive school, they expected me to work, not be frivolous with my time. If I persisted in my foolish behavior, I could transfer to the University of Vermont where at least I would not be wasting their money.

Crying hysterically, I returned to my room. I threw the cushions Mother had made for our flea market sofa and chairs onto the floor and stomped on them. Her demand seemed unreasonable, but what if she were right? Her call reinforced all of my insecurities. I raged and worried. Was it possible not to study every weekend and still keep my grades up to the required level? My roommate kept to one end of her bed, while my hallmates clustered at the door. They told me I should just ignore my mother. Her demand was ridiculous.

I agreed with them, but I didn't know how to tell her. I made an appointment with the college shrink, hoping he would say my mother was wrong. I wanted him to tell me that I had every right to date and to go away for weekends. He didn't. He asked me how I felt about my mother's ultimatum. What about it seemed to *me* to be unreasonable? What did I plan to do? I had no answers for him. Disappointed that he wouldn't give me permission to do what I wanted to do, I left his office. Soon thereafter, in time for a long-anticipated weekend at Hamilton College, I made my own decision. Lying was the only way to proceed.

Lying by omission or commission became my standard practice. Day trips to New York City were expensive and meant time away from my studies. Mother didn't hear about my ecstatic discovery of the Metropolitan Museum, the coffee shops in Greenwich Village, the belly dancing palaces on Eighth Avenue, or the pleasures of Washington Square. I simply neglected to mention them in my letters. Weekends at Hamilton were more problematic. Not only was I lying about where I was, but wading drunkenly through ankle-deep beer on my way to the darkened "pit" with my date was not on Mother's list of acceptable activities. I persisted in doing what I wanted to do, but guilt never left me.

So I told no one but Andy of my financial predicament. Knowing my mother, he thought my decision perfectly understandable.

Towards the end of the third day of my vagabondage, I carried my luggage across the street from the main campus to the lawn of Alumnae House. There I concealed it beneath some shrubbery. Alumnae House was the college hotel and home to the beloved Pub, the snack and coffee shop where, with money in my pocket, I had wasted many hours during the previous year. This move made me more nervous than ever, afraid that someone would recognize me and ask what in the world I was doing here and, horrible to contemplate, contact my mother. By this time my clothes were quite grubby and I was very hungry. What if Andy didn't come after all? What would I do then?

Towards evening the familiar blue Ford pulled up the driveway. I don't think I have ever liked my brother quite as much as I did that day. He even bought me a hamburger in the Pub, the best of my life. My story safe in his hands, we set off for Burlington in the warmth and luxury of a car.

I decided early on that honesty was not a successful strategy in dealing with my mother. I was sure my parents would be disappointed if they were to learn who or what I was.

Poetry, when I finally came to write it after both were dead, provides me a way to say what I really feel and think, to blurt out the previously concealed.

27 ❖ Maud Nuquist: My People

1961 and 1966

In 1961 I was twenty and my Grandmother Maud seventy-eight when we shared a hotel room in Cleveland. My brother was receiving an m.s. degree from the School of Applied Social Science at Western Reserve. Maud, for whom education was of major importance, attended graduations of every one of her seven grandchildren.

I had lately become used to, rather almost expected, admiring glances. For the three days we were together, I might as well have been invisible. As Grandmother made her way down hallways, through lobbies, in and out of elevators or restaurants, people stepped aside as though she were a queen. Could she really not have noticed how people scurried to open doors, to stand aside as she passed? Was she oblivious to the stares? I tried to understand. She was a large woman, tall, with a mass of carefully combed thick white hair worn rolled at the neck. She wore her good jewelry, her dark lace dresses, and, dare I say, affected an air of modest but stately humility. Walking behind her, enchanted, I watched her carefully.

On a visit to Burlington in 1966 Maud told her story to my mother, who wrote it down. I confirmed the details by searching libraries and church, county, and state records. Mother admired and respected her mother-in-law Maud more than any other woman. Maud was capable, energetic, idealistic, and ambitious (although she would never admit, even to herself, the latter).

Maud

Mama and Papa came out to Nebraska from Ohio in May of 1875. They traveled by wagon from Mama's farm in Bern Township to Portsmouth, where they stayed overnight with Mama's brother, George Selby. Uncle George was selling sewing machines for the

Singer Company and already was very successful, even then, before he began his shoe business. Uncle George had the idea to make shoes on a production line, a newfangled idea at the time. I think Papa always measured himself against Uncle George, but poor Papa had no talent for capitalism nor any particular interest in technology, Uncle George's passion. Uncle George's fine home in the city was quite a contrast to what they were about to find in Nebraska.

The next day Mama and Papa took the train to Cincinnati and changed trains there to begin the thirty-five hour journey to Omaha on the Baltimore and Ohio Line. In Omaha they changed trains once more for the trip to Plum Creek, Nebraska. There they unloaded their few possessions in a heavy May snowstorm. They hired a wagon to drive them forty slippery miles through falling snow to their claim on the Republican River near Arapahoe. When at last they arrived, there wasn't much to see. Just the river, the dirt palisades above the river, and endless miles of prairie buried under snow.

I've often tried to imagine Mama at the moment the wagon left them — cold, tired, no people or buildings in sight, no place to rest or shelter except what they could provide for themselves. Fortunately both Mama and Papa had grown up on farms. They were big strong people used to working with their hands, and they were young.

Within a day the snow melted. Papa cut dugouts into the hillside by the river, one for them to live in and a small one for storage beside it.

On a morning that first spring, Papa and Mama awoke to discover a band of Pawnee clustered around the entrance of the storage dugout. They weren't there to take anything but to leave something— one of their young men was lying on his buffalo skin in the corner, too ill with smallpox to go on. Mama kept the Indian fed and warm, and he survived. A few weeks later when the Pawnee came back to find the young man's burial site, he greeted them, scarred, weak, but on the mend.

In gratitude, the Indians told Papa it was forbidden to live so near the river. They insisted he move to higher ground. They wouldn't leave until he had cut squares of sod and built a one-room house set well back from the water. Years and years later, in 1937, when the Pawnee were long gone from those lands, a flash flood destroyed many homes along the Republican, but the site of the old homestead was well above the water.

Papa managed to break ground and do a little planting, despite not having a horse to help cut through the heavy sod. But then, after that May snowfall, it didn't snow or rain again. The crops died and grasshoppers came and ate up whatever was left. Papa found work as a well digger.

He earned enough to provide food for the winter and to buy seed for spring planting. He plowed ground for Mama to make a vegetable garden near the soddy. Mama was expecting a baby, but she still managed to lug water up from the river to keep the garden growing.

But the grasshoppers came again. They turned the sky dark and covered the ground with a thick crawling carpet. They ate the ground bare and then they ate the carrots and onions and beets under the ground. Papa went back to well digging.

At the end of October, he was out working with a crew, miles from the soddy, when he was sure he heard Mama call his name, "Joe, Joe!" All he said to the foreman was "Jennie needs me," and he set out across the prairie towards home. He walked all day. Any rivulet or spring where he might have hoped to get a drink was clogged full of dead grasshoppers.

Mama did need him. She had been in labor since the night before, alone there in the soddy. Papa tried to help her, but by morning it was clear that things weren't going right. He could see that Mama needed a doctor. Papa left her again and walked to Kansas. It took most of a day to find a doctor. By the time they returned in the doctor's rig, Mama had labored all alone for most of two nights and two days. It was another full day after the doctor arrived when, at last, my sister Blanche was born.

All the skin on the top of Blanche's head was worn off from that long struggle. For months the large abscess that formed wouldn't heal. Blanche's little hands kept picking at it. Mama's folks sent out some salve on the train from Ohio. Papa drove his newly acquired horse and wagon all the way back to Plum Creek to pick up that medicine.

Mama crocheted the dearest little pair of mittens with drawstrings around the wrists to keep Blanche from pulling off the scabs. Blanche never saved things like I do. After Mama died, Blanche didn't want the mittens, but I kept them.

It was after Blanche was born that Mama began to have her sick headaches. Mama's people back in Ohio were worried about her, so they sent Mama's older sister, Mehetable Tabitha Selby, out to greet the new baby and to see for herself about this homesteading business. Papa was proud to be able to fetch her in his new wagon, drawn by his new horse. Aunt Bith was not much impressed by it, or by anything else.

One day Aunt Bith and Mama were inside, sitting in the buffalo hide and hickory chairs Papa had made, sewing. An enormous bull snake fell down out of the sod onto Aunt Bith's lap. She leapt up shrieking. Mama somehow managed to prod the snake out the door as it coiled and writhed around her broom handle. It was as fat as her arm and three times as long. Aunt Bith stood in the middle of the room, watching the ceiling, shuddering, her shaking hands clenched at her bosom. Mama couldn't calm her or get her to sit down.

When Aunt Bith could move, she snatched up her valise, examined it to make sure there weren't any snakes looped around it, and began to pack. Still trembling, she demanded to know how Mama could stand it. This wasn't a fit place for anyone to live. Mama should pack up, too. If she wouldn't leave on her own account, Mama should at least consider the poor baby. What if that thing had fallen on Blanche?

Mama tried to talk to her. That snake was harmless. It wouldn't hurt anybody. It helped keep the mice down. It was gone now and Bith shouldn't worry about it anymore. Wouldn't she just sit down and have a cup of tea? She'd feel better.

When Aunt Bith had her things stuffed into the valise, she dragged it right out the door. She wouldn't be deterred. She was headed for the train station, forty miles away.

Aunt Bith had been gone for several hours by the time Papa got home. Mama sent him out to look for her. When he found her, she was dusty and bedraggled but still walking. She refused to stop or to get in the wagon. Papa rode along beside her for awhile, but she just shook her head at everything he said. Only after he promised he wouldn't make her go back to the homestead, but would drive her directly to the train station in Plum Creek did she let herself be helped aboard.

Mama and Papa stayed in Furnas County for seven years. Papa never did manage to harvest a crop. And Papa grew up on a farm, a

good farm, near Chesterhill, Ohio, but this wasn't any kind of farming
he could understand.

The Edgerton family had farmed in this country for two hundred
years by that time, first in New Jersey, then in North Carolina, then
in Ohio, and now in Nebraska. His people had always been part of
a group of Quakers who moved together since they first fled from
persecution in England, but now Papa wasn't part of a group anymore.
He and Mama had moved by themselves.

Papa's family left North Carolina in 1804 with other Quakers who
decided it was wrong to live in a place that permitted slavery. Papa's
parents were very strict and conservative. They opposed all political
groups, because political groups always meant compromise. They
didn't believe in compromise. They would give aid to an individual
runaway slave. They could not join or approve of the Anti-Slavery
Society of Friends, although one of Grandpa Edgerton's brothers was
a founder of that society.

The Quaker community was split apart, first over the issue of how
to witness against slavery, and then by the Civil War.

When war came, Grandma and Grandpa Edgerton brought two
books home from the Friends' library kept in the Chesterhill Meeting
House. They were *Reasons for the Silent Waiting* by Mary Brook and *An
Inquiry into the Accordance of War with the Principles of Christianity* by
Jonathan Dymond. Papa remembered Grandpa reading them aloud
after evening devotions, and the family's passionate discussions
about the calls of duty and conscience. In the end Papa's parents held
fast to the old ways. Grandpa's brother was disowned by the meeting,
as were all the young men who went off to fight.

Papa was just a boy then. Perhaps he learned the wrong lessons
from those days. He learned to follow only the prompting of his own
heart and conscience. When his older sister married a non-Quaker
"out of the meeting," he, unlike his parents, attended her wedding.
The committee appointed to "treat with him" reported that it "did not
think him in a suitable disposition of mind to condemn his deviations"
and, on the 17th day of the fourth month of 1875, recommended he be
disowned.

Perhaps his unsuitable disposition could be explained by more
than his love of his sister. He was already set to leave for Nebraska less

than two weeks after his "treatment," and he had married Mama the year before despite her being the daughter of a Universalist.

Mama, Sarah Jane "Jennie" Selby, had many older brothers and sisters. Her father did not have need of a farmhand. Papa no longer had a position or a future with his own family in Chesterhill. That is when Papa and Mama decided to take up a claim in Nebraska.

Once there, it didn't take Papa long to decide there were more satisfactory ways to earn a living than to try to raise crops where grasshoppers were more certain than rain. He continued to work occasionally at drilling wells, but he became a clerk for W.S. Morlan, an attorney in Arapahoe, and read law there in that office. He passed his bar exams and set up in business for himself.

Papa felt he had been lucky to give up on farming as soon as he did. Well drilling and clerking hadn't paid much, but they gave him time to read law. It prevented him from going deeper into debt. He was lucky, too, that after Aunt Bith's visit, Mama's people sent out supplies—cloth and staples and special treats for the baby. Most of the settlers didn't have comfortably situated families back in Ohio to help out. Most of them either had to make good on their claims or lose everything—and many people did lose everything.

Papa saw good people trained to farming like himself, without capital like himself, go deeper and deeper into debt. They took out chattel mortgages on wagons, plows, and even on their oxen and their mules. They obtained second and third mortgages on their land, even as interest rates rose. If they did manage to raise a crop, railroad rates were so high they lost money shipping it to market. The paperwork involved when people gave up hope and abandoned their claims made up a lot of Papa's business.

Papa had been a Republican because it was the party that abolished slavery, but on September 20, 1879, he took his first step into radical politics. The year 1879 was especially hard on farmers. They took out mortgages when prices were high and now had to pay them back with crops that were worth less and less. He attended a meeting in Beaver City called by "many voters" to nominate a county ticket which would represent "all earnest free men ... greenbackers, labor and reform elements ... all who oppose contraction and the National banking system ... who desire the establishment of a paper money by the government equal with coin as legal tender for all debts, public and private, and for the full and free coinage of silver! All who favor economy in public affairs, and oppose extravagant official salaries! All who believe in the sovereignty of the people and the people's money."

After attending that Greenback party convention, Papa never looked back. For the rest of his life, Papa pushed for laws that benefited all and didn't enrich some on the backs and arms of the many. In other words, he turned his back on the Republican Party.

In 1882, Papa read an ad in the *Arapahoe Pioneer*. The Swedish settlement of Stromsburg was looking for a lawyer who could read and write in English to prepare a town charter. The community hoped the lawyer would be sympathetic to its populist values. The position suited him. Stromsburg was socially conservative but politically radical which also described Papa, a teetotaler who believed in the equitable distribution of wealth.

So, leaving the soddy and the homemade furniture behind, he and Mama and Blanche moved to Stromsburg. My twin sister, Mabel, and I were born there soon after. Mabel only lived for eight days.

Although I rarely think about her, sometimes I've wondered if my entire life has been a search for her, the intimate womb companion of my first nine months. It seemed to me I long for something missing, a closeness I have never found. Could Mabel be another explanation for my difficulty in expressing my feelings, my stiffness? Oh, nonsense.

Papa prospered in Stromsburg and soon had a frame house built for Mama, my sister Blanche, and me. He was proud of the Brussels carpet in the parlor, the store-bought walnut furniture, and the base burner stove with its automatic coal feed. I played across the road in the town square where new trees had recently replaced tall prairie grass. Above our front door was a round window, blue and red stained glass, an eye keeping watch over me.

I was unhappy in 1887 when we moved away and rented a house in South Omaha. South Omaha was a new city of mud, smoke, stockyards, railyards, odd smells and languages, and women in babushkas wearing torn and flapping shoes. It seemed ugly to me, huge, noisy, and frightening.

I knew Mama missed our house in Stromsburg, too, but she explained that Papa had come to South Omaha to represent the

Knights of Labor in their struggle for a better life. She told me it was important for the workers to have an attorney stand up for their rights.

She was proud of my father's political life as a member of the Nebraska Farmers' Alliance and as an early Populist Party leader. My parents' conversation was full of issues and possibilities, the eight-hour day, the need to regulate railroad rates for the farmers' benefit, and the dangers of the falling price of wheat. My older sister, Blanche, was bored by this talk, and my baby brother, Edgar, was too young to follow it, but from the very beginning I was swept into the swirl of hope that surrounded my father in those years.

My interest mirrored my mother's. Although as a woman she couldn't vote, and it was considered improper for her to participate actively in a campaign, she served as Papa's sounding board. Her good sense helped him clarify his arguments. One plank of the Populist platform was to urge the vote for women. Populists were much derided for such a stand, but not by my mother.

The first time Papa ran for office was in 1887 when the Union Labor Party needed a candidate for the Nebraska Supreme Court on its ticket, and he was the only attorney who supported the Union Labor cause. He was the Union Labor candidate for the United States Congress in 1888, the Populist candidate for Nebraska attorney general in 1890, and the Populist candidate for the Supreme Court in 1891. Again and again I was disappointed by his defeats—the elections he lost by wide margins, as well as the ones he almost won.

During my father's campaigns, because of Mother's steady support and her explanation of the interests arrayed against him, I could bear to read the newspapers that said such bad things about him. I was sure those things weren't true:

> Edgerton's election would be the greatest calamity ever to befall
> Nebraska!
> Edgerton unfit to serve as dogcatcher, his campaign is a black mark on
> the history of our state.
> Edgerton has failed at everything he's tried, from farming to lawyering,
> and now he wants our vote.

We moved twice more by 1891. Soon I grew anxious when Papa came home excited about anything, because that excitement often led to our trunks and barrels being pulled out and packed up again. Blanche and little Edgar and I would have to begin again to make new friends and to settle into a new school. It was never clear to me that for Papa the place we came to was better than the place we left. Even Mama finally said that Papa was not a practical man, but until I was twelve, I continued to believe that Papa was the kindest, best-intentioned, smartest father a girl could have. After he spoke to the newspaper man about Blanche's elopement, I still knew he was a good person but I lost some confidence in his judgment.

I know my interest in public life was awakened in my childhood. I could never have guessed then that in another time of turmoil, the Great Depression, I would become a candidate myself. Through studies conducted by the Nebraska Women's Clubs, I was appalled to learn of the medieval conditions prevailing in Nebraska's prisons and juvenile facilities and the dearth of programs to assist the growing numbers of the destitute in our state. Failing to get the attention of the politicians then in power, I entered the 1934 Nebraska Democratic Primary as a candidate for the office of governor, the first woman ever to do so.

Like my father, I was unsuccessful, but the issues I raised did become part of the public debate. Papa, by example, taught me to stand up for my beliefs despite the personal cost.

Maud 1966

Pride was my weakness and when
pride was not justified by facts,
I worked to conceal the facts.
I wanted so much.

I wanted my father to be elected
to Congress,
to be made a judge
of the Nebraska Supreme Court.
It took time to admit to myself
that he did not, perhaps,
have the qualifications of judgment
and temperament to be elected.

I wanted my sons to be national leaders.
I wanted my daughter to be beautiful
as well as smart. Now I can admit
the failure of those hopes. My daughter
was the smartest of all the children,
a Phi Beta Kappa, but she was not beautiful
and she soon married a man who loved her
but was thoughtless of her needs.

My youngest son was caught in a disgraceful
homosexual scandal. I sent him to a mental
hospital to be straightened out. No more scandals
but no more law career either, and I'm afraid
his predilections remained unchanged. I know
he loved me very much. In many ways he was
the most faithful of them all, but always
so much secrecy, so much to conceal.

The middle boy, book-smart, suffered
from epilepsy and a violent temper.
He was my constant worry and my grief.
I always blamed the doctor, his careless
use of forceps, for my son's trouble, while
for some reason my son blamed me. He
was very unstable, never did complete
his Ph.D. He died in a fire in Chicago
trying to save a life, the best thing he ever
did, his last. It is painful to think
about his life, his death.

My oldest child, my most beloved son, moved
so far away. A professor, he did well, I guess,
although not as I had hoped, not on the national
stage. But he was too removed to ask my
advice or even to know what my advice
might have been.

My marriage was a good one in most ways.
My husband, although his parents were from Sweden,

was well-thought of (although a little
feared). A good and honest businessman,
an enormous man in size and strength and heart,
he wasn't much interested in life outside our
state or, in his later years, in politics, but he
always respected my endeavors, never held me
back when I was elected to the board
of the National Federation of Women's Clubs
and traveled so much nor when I ran
for governor or was appointed to the Nebraska
Board of Control. I know he wished I were more
interested in the physical side of marriage, but I
did give him four children and thought that
quite enough.

I don't know how I feel about my life.
I could have done more. There was always
satisfaction in work—whether baking pies
or studying the dreadful conditions in the girls'
reformatory. Now the name of Nuquist
doesn't mean much anymore, my husband dead,
my children not what I had hoped,
my health deteriorating,

I am ready to be done with it.

28 ❖ Vassar Virgins

Poughkeepsie, New York, 1959–1962

Sadly, technically speaking, I was one, more or less, on April 4, 1962, when President Sarah Gibson Blanding gave her famous speech. No one knew why we had been abruptly summoned to the chapel for this unusual all-school compulsory evening gathering. After a brief announcement and explanation of the need to increase fees for the following year, Miss Blanding, her hair in its usual bun and her saddle shoes firm on her feet, surprised us. She launched into a stern denunciation of premarital sex and excessive drinking. She told us neither would be tolerated at Vassar. Disciplinary action would be taken against those who did not follow the "innate standards" of the college. We sat in embarrassed astonishment as Miss Blanding declared that promiscuity was indecent and immoral. She advised those students who could not follow the rules to withdraw voluntarily from the school, before they were asked to leave. Virginity and temperance were required of Vassar students.

I wondered how they would know for sure who had broken the code. Would we be summoned to the Warden's office to swear that we were neither wantons nor drunks? If we were already indecent or immoral how could they rely on us to adhere to Vassar's honor system? Were we all to have a mandatory gynecological exam? What a horror—to spread my legs before the infirmary doctors and nurses.

We had all already endured one unbelievable breach of privacy—the "posture pictures" which were mandatory for every incoming freshman. One at a time, stripped naked, we had been made to enter an empty room where a voice directed us to stand just so, to turn to the right, to the left, while someone took photographs of us. Mercifully we couldn't see the photographer, but, shivering and humiliated, we wondered who was on the other side of the camera.

How many people would look at these pictures? Where were they kept? We were told, of course, that they would be handled with discretion, but what did that mean exactly?

The purpose of these pictures, supposedly, was to determine any faults of posture which could then be addressed and corrected in an amazing course called "Freshmen Fundamentals." In "Fundies," as the course was dubbed by its unwilling participants, we were taught how to sit gracefully, stand elegantly, walk fluidly, and most important of all, how to lift a suitcase correctly onto the luggage rack of a train. We strove, of course, for perfect posture in each movement.

One of my hall mates, her small frame muscled and taut from prep school softball, was assigned, much to her disgust, to *Remedial* Fundamentals when it was determined her hamstrings were too tight. In Remedial Fundamentals, learning to keep one's knees together and ankles crossed while seated was supplemented by additional hours of stretching and flexing.

But what had caused the president's sudden outrage? Had she discovered someone *in flagrante delicto*? Did she really expect seniors with less than two months until graduation to confess and to leave without a diploma? As far as I could remember, our handbooks had not said Vassar was for virgins only.

As incoming freshmen, we had learned from the sophomores and juniors in our dormitories that a man's jacket hanging on a closed door meant, "Do Not Knock. Do Not Enter. Do Not Ask What is Happening in This Room." As long as the door was closed, fornication apparently wasn't anyone's business except the participants'. It didn't seem fair for the president to be stating an anti-fornication policy retroactively.

When we were freshmen, the warden had told us in an orientation lecture that Vassar considered the custom of going off on weekends to men's schools a valid part of student life. These weekends were more or less unsupervised fraternity debauches. Had the college really been unaware of what had been going on both on campus and off?

Lord knows there were plenty of unpleasant possible consequences that carried their own grim punishments. The fear of pregnancy and venereal disease was sufficient to frighten many of us into some sort of self-restraint. Religious conviction prevented others from "going all the way." Nothing, however, was sufficient to keep us all from the pleasures, mysteries, and misadventures of sex.

And what about "excessive drinking"? Alcohol was not allowed on campus or in the dormitories. Those rules were pretty well respected. We did our drinking off campus, legally, since eighteen was the legal age for drinking in New York State at that time. I *had* watched a very drunken girl throw up all over our housefather's shoes once. As freshmen, a group of us, having consumed the Gallo port we carried in our wineskins (a most sophisticated *accoutrement*, we thought), went swimming in our underwear in the drainage creek behind the faculty apartments. Sophomore year the handbook added the creek to the territory to be kept alcohol-free. But surely, I thought guiltily, that freshman indiscretion could not be the cause of this chastisement.

Excessive drinking was harder to conceal than lack of virginity. Looking around, I really couldn't tell who was a virgin and who was not, whereas a drunk would have been detectable by the smell, if by nothing else. Of course, for the most part we knew such facts about one another. We knew who returned hungover from weekends (most of us, if truth be told). We knew who had succumbed to the importuning of a fiancé with much misgiving and subsequent guilt. We knew who hung out at the "townie" bars and gaily rode away on motorcycles clinging to the back of a tee-shirted stranger. We suffered pangs of jealousy at the pretty and willing among us who went off with the Kingston Trio after its on-campus concert. We knew, or suspected we knew, those who had had abortions. We knew, more or less, who was spared the temptations of sex with a man by a preference for sex with women. Was sex with a woman premarital sex? Was it promiscuity? Until Miss Blanding's lecture, we had considered our behavior to be a private matter of conscience or appetite or hope or despair.

The aftermath of the speech was really rather unpleasant, pitting the unfallen against the fallen, the good against the wicked, in bitter argument. A college poll of 1,040 students out of a total student population of 1,450 concluded that fifty-two percent of us agreed with Miss Blanding that we should be pure and temperate. Forty percent of us disagreed. The rest of us were undecided.

We were further embarrassed by prurient reporters asking impertinent personal questions. Most of us scuttled to classes, trying to avoid them, but every major newspaper and magazine wrote stories about us and about our reaction to President Blanding's surprise.

However, the poll contained an additional proposition: "Social morals are a personal matter that should be of concern to the college only when they bring the name of Vassar into public disrepute." Eighty-one percent of us agreed. This was perhaps a portent. Although I voted for privacy along with eighty-one percent of my fellow students, I sometimes thought it might be pleasant to have no choices, for rules to be so explicit and generally accepted, that no moral decisions remained to be made. I was only slowly stumbling into the autonomy of adulthood.

Apparently Miss Blanding's speech was more of a *cri de coeur,* a last blast from a fading moral position, than an actual statement of policy. As far as I know, no moral delinquents were drummed out of school. None of us was summoned to an inquisition. I'm quite sure future handbooks did not state virginity as a necessary condition for admission.

Within two years Miss Blanding had retired. The social revolution of the late 1960s and early 1970s rendered her speech quaint, dear, and irrelevant. Soon after Miss Blanding left Vassar, the student movement dismantled the concept of *in loco parentis.* Then Vassar and its dormitories became co-ed. For a few gaudy years, until some sort of balance was restored, I've heard that many young women felt like prey in a hunting preserve. In 1962 drugs had still been a rumor. We had heard of marijuana, but only a tiny minority, the truly rebellious, had tried it.

I don't know how any young woman negotiates the pressures of freedom these days. I had enough trouble making my way in my own less complicated era. From what I read "hooking up" is unproblematic to the majority. It would terrify me.

SECTION SEVEN
A Temporary Reality

29 ❖ Wedding

1962

Imet Arturo at Basin Harbor Club, a resort on Lake Champlain, the summer following my sophomore year. I was a waitress; he wrote and illustrated the resort's daily information sheet and designed and painted its signs.

He was immediately the center of staff get-to-gathers after the end of our evening shifts. Twenty-nine years old, dark and good-looking, he flirted with all the girls, and seemed to enjoy being the center of attention.

I wasn't drawn to him at first. My father's serious demeanor was what I was used to in a man, but Arturo focused his attention on me. He began to tell me wonderful stories. He emigrated from Cuba in 1953 and had lived in New York City since then. About to finish a course in interior design at Parsons, he loved New York as much as I did.

Arturo told me about his life in Cuba, growing up in the center of Havana in his grandfather's enormous old house large enough for his parents and his aunts and uncles to have private quarters.

He told stories about his family's beach house in Veradero, his teaching in an elementary school, the processions and flowers on Holy Saturday, ice cream made from tropical fruits I had never heard the names of before, his father's fainting away when he learned that Arturo had contracted polio, and his years of daily swim therapy as the Sister Kenny method prescribed. Arturo was extremely self-conscious about the resulting atrophy of his left leg. I felt honored that he shared such a difficult personal detail about himself.

By the end of the summer we had spent many evening hours lying on a blanket under the northern lights, kissing and talking. We began to speak in general terms about marriage.

It seemed as important to him as to my parents that I be a virgin at marriage. I thought his willingness to wait showed his maturity in contrast to some of the dates I had fought off the previous couple of years.

Arturo was drawn to me because I didn't drive and didn't smoke, not despite those failings. He didn't like aggressive women. He loved me for my femininity and sweet docility. I'd worried all through school that I was too assertive in class, too fond of sports, and too tall, so I was pleased to discover I was actually acceptably feminine and passive. I grew my hair long and coiled it in a heavy bun that, according to Arturo, made me appear a true Spanish *maja*.

In the fall I took the train into the City to visit him as often as I could manage. I began to think more seriously about marrying him. He would be successful, and we would lead a glamorous life in Manhattan. We both enjoyed museums, the theater, ballet, exploring the city.

That winter his parents, aunt and uncle, and his cousins with their two young daughters fled Castro's Cuba. They all moved into Arturo's small railroad flat on 96th Street. They were forced to leave everything behind—jobs, houses, cars, money—but the family had contacts in New York and managed to find temporary work sufficient for food and winter coats. I admired the effort that let them get along together.

I was invited to many jolly meals—roast pork or *picadillo*, rice and black beans, *plátanos fritos*, avocado and grapefruit salad, and flan. The noise and general *jaleo* of those family gatherings were certainly different from the quiet dinners at home. Arturo's mother, Armanda, did most of the cooking.

I liked Armanda right away. As a girl she boarded in a convent school outside New York City and her English was excellent. Back in Havana she had a long career in the Ministry of Education, unusual for a woman in those days. Despite being a serious person, she married an unofficial dance king of Havana, Arturo's father, also named Arturo. She was the practical, forceful partner who kept the marriage together through all its ups and downs.

That spring when Arturo asked me to marry him, I said yes. For the announcement of the engagement both sets of parents came to Vassar. Arturo's parents took the train out to Poughkeepsie while my parents drove down from Vermont. It was a beautiful spring day, the campus in full bloom, my roommates congratulatory. The celebratory dinner my parents hosted at a local restaurant was amiable. Although Arturo's father spoke almost no English, our parents seemed disposed to be friends.

Much to my surprise, upon his graduation, Arturo announced he had taken a job at a furniture store in Iowa. Iowa? Why Iowa? Couldn't he find a job in New York City? What about our plans? He told me he wanted to learn more about his adopted country. It would be an adventure.

Well, okay. Mother had lived in Iowa as a girl—perhaps I would be exploring my roots.

I saw Arturo only once my senior year. We corresponded almost daily. He seemed to enjoy life in Iowa, exotic to his prior experience. I was disappointed we wouldn't be living in New York City as I had expected.

Many of the more talented members of my class who announced their engagements were drawn aside by their professors, their women professors especially, who asked them if they were certain they were doing the right thing, throwing away their chances for graduate school and careers. Perhaps in his absence my commitment to Arturo had become a little tenuous since I did think I might be ready to break my engagement if anyone asked me such a question. I would find a way to go on to study international relations. *My* professors, however, simply congratulated me on my upcoming marriage, confirming my doubts about my capabilities. In those days marriage was still a respectable career path.

When I broached my desire for a career in the Foreign Service to my mother, she said she didn't think it appropriate. An unmarried woman posted out of the country would be vulnerable to affairs and, inevitably, the subject of gossip.

> If I had joined the State Department instead
> of becoming a lady, perhaps I would
> have written memos. Because I always
> had ladylike tendencies, I would have
> worked hard to reconcile opposing opinions.
> I would exist in State as the creature
> of someone else's imagination.

My father never hired a woman to teach in his department. I heard him say women would make the men uncomfortable, would cause disturbances of one kind or another. My father insisted I get my degree in liberal arts. He opposed "vocational training" such as education courses, a business degree, or anything that would prepare me for an actual job.

My parents' ambition for me was that I pass from virginity to marriage with no scandal in between.

It was fine for a woman to be educated, if she put her education to use on behalf of her husband, to be his helpmeet and sounding board, just as my mother, once married to him, had served my father. They wondered if Arturo was sufficiently solid to be the one to whom I should devote my efforts. Why was a thirty-one year old man not more firmly established in his profession? I defended him to them and to myself, brushed aside their doubts. He'd gone to Parsons to give himself more opportunities. I knew they approved of education.

Then in the spring, Arturo left Iowa for a job in High Point, North Carolina, designing rooms to appear in advertisements and magazine articles for a photographic studio. We wouldn't be living in Iowa after all—another jolt, another change to contemplate.

The wedding, two weeks after my graduation, was in our church in Burlington, the First Congregational. Even after ten years in New York, Arturo's accent was indecipherable to Grandmother Nuquist and Granddaddy Wilson. I could feel their polite skepticism but at twenty-one, I was sure I knew best. Alas, my dear Grandmother Wilson had died the year before. When I brought Arturo to Burlington on my day off from Basin Harbor Club to meet the family, she was quite taken with Arturo's charm and prepossession and, today, would have been happy for me.

Shortly after Grandmother met Arturo, she had a series of abdominal surgeries to relieve exactly what condition I was never told and then quickly sank into a gentle dementia. Granddaddy found caring for her a heavy burden—one that required a great deal of assistance from my mother. I was away at school when, at Mother's insistence, Grandmother was transferred to a nursing home a short distance away on South Union Street.

Then Mother urged Granddaddy to get away for a while to visit his son in Long Island. Reluctantly he agreed. That was how things stood upon my return home from Vassar in May 1961.

On my twice-daily visits, accompanied by Mother in the morning and on my own in the afternoon, I found Grandmother sweetly befuddled. She asked plaintively again and again for Granddaddy. "Where is Walter?" "I wish I could see Walter."

One afternoon I urged Grandmother to let me do something for her, anything at all.

"Well," she said, "I could drink a glass of milk. I always did fancy a glass of milk."

I went in search of an attendant only to be told that it would soon be time for supper and my grandmother could have a glass of milk then if she still wanted it. No, it wouldn't be possible for her to have one now. It wasn't on the schedule.

All my grandmother wanted of me was a glass of milk and I couldn't even give her that. While I repeated what the attendant had said, I couldn't hide my distress. Grandmother observed my tears and apologized to *me* for being a bother.

I cried on my short walk home. Still crying I went to Mother, told her about the milk. "Can't we please bring Grandmother home? I promise I'll help take care of her."

Mother, herself suffering from a guilty conscience, agreed. She would make the arrangements.

The phone rang early the next morning. Grandmother was dead. I knew it was because she thought her Walter was gone forever and she didn't want to be a trouble to the rest of us.

Granddaddy never forgave himself for not being with her when she died. None of us could speak of her having died alone.

But today, although I missed Grandmother's gentle presence, was not a day for grief. The wedding ceremony complete, we all assembled for fruit punch and cake in the community room of the church. Arturo's family no doubt wondered about the short and simple Protestant service, the lack of music, food, and dancing, but appeared cheerful and pleased about the marriage.

After a picnic in the backyard of Cliff Street, we drove off in the late afternoon in our new white Corvair. We crammed as many wedding presents as we could into the car and arranged for the rest to be shipped. Our honeymoon was to be the three-day drive from my family's home in Burlington to High Point.

So clearly prepared for the challenges ahead and as docilely as possible, I set off in my new tangerine polyester dress with the tiny waist Mother sewed for the occasion. At my side, beautiful Arturo.

We reached Saratoga Springs in the long June twilight and found our way to a guesthouse. Cascades of rice fell from our clothes as we stepped out of the car. More rice fell in a little white circle around each of us while Arturo inquired about accommodations. With a wink and a leering smile, the proprietor led us upstairs to a room where a chenille-covered double bed seemed to call embarrassing attention to itself.

After dinner at a restaurant recommended by the innkeeper, we returned to our room. I used the bathroom first. I struggled to insert my brand-new diaphragm, very springy and resistant. I changed into my new nightgown and robe, virginal white cotton, sheer and ruffly, a fine mix of innocence and provocation, I thought.

While Arturo used the bathroom, I arranged myself as fetchingly as possible on the bed, my dark hair spread out on the pillow, my white gown graceful around me. Irresistible, I hoped, especially to one who had been waiting as long for me as I for him.

Arturo had told me he disliked pushy women and that, especially in sex, I was never to be the instigator but to wait for him to take the lead. If he got things started all would be well; otherwise he had a little impotence problem. Not knowing any better, I didn't see that as a difficulty. In the time we had been together, he had always seemed to be full of desire for me, although we had stopped short of intercourse. Now, at last, it was finally okay to "do it."

Arturo came to bed. After some kisses that seemed passionate Arturo said "I'm very tired. Aren't you? It's been a long day." He fluffed his pillow, turned off the light and rolled away on to his side.

I couldn't believe it. I lay there wide-awake in the dark. I began to suspect I had made a terrible mistake. The word "annulment" rose to my mind. I couldn't let myself think that way. Until death do us part. Promises made. It *had* been a long day. Perhaps he thought he was being considerate. And I began to rationalize. What was I? Some sort of sex fiend? I just needed to be patient. Arturo thought I was beautiful. He had said so. He was attracted to me. Everything would be fine.

Two more nights, two more motels. The marriage remained unconsummated. I felt my inexperience. What could I do? What should I do? What did it mean? Several days after we reached High Point the deed was done. By then all spontaneity, all joyful anticipation had been replaced by self-conscious anxiety. Would I say something, or do something, or want something that would make him withdraw again? My fears diminished when, once begun, he seemed almost as eager as I was.

Then, just like that, sex stopped.

The first few weeks of that summer, I relearned loneliness. Now sex, or the lack thereof, my greatest worry, my big concern, was the thing I could not talk about with anyone, especially my husband, the only person I knew in North Carolina. During college I talked everything over, freely and frankly, with my female friends. I was raised to believe, however, that without exception, the secrets of marriage were to be kept between a husband and wife. No doubt pride, too, kept me from speaking. I didn't want anyone to know the truth of what I began to fear was a sham marriage.

My life had certainly changed: one month, intellectually charged and challenged; the next month, enduring long boiling hot days with nothing to do. The one constant in both lives was sexual frustration. By fall I obtained an underpaid secretarial job in the office of Pittsburgh Plate Glass that at least kept me occupied during the day. No one in High Point seemed impressed by my Vassar degree.

On Behalf of Machismo

Hints and omens
I didn't read. Often
at parties we the only
straight couple,
or so I thought.
He danced, told
funny stories, kept
us all away.

He lived behind a mask.
If his dreams
could be made real
by hiding and denying,
it was worth the price.

Months and years
without sex.
Now, I understand
how desperate he was
to keep himself
even from himself.

Then, what I felt
was abandoned.

This has been a difficult chapter to write. A friend who read it wrote something so helpful to me. She said, "Maybe you and Arturo were perfectly matched in how you *paced* yourselves and each other—in not breaking away from your conditioning too fast and living your passionate sexuality too fast. You gradually lived into your truths."

30 ❖ High Point

1962

Looking out over the High Point Kiwanis Club in the early winter of 1962, I was very aware of being the only woman and, at twenty-one, the youngest person in the room. About to begin my speech, I tried to take deep breaths and ignore my wobbly knees.

In some families it is expected that everyone will play tennis, or drink too much, or act in plays, or become a doctor. In our family, we were all expected to give speeches. Even Grandmother Wilson, shy as she was, had led devotions or given a report on a chapter of the Bible to the Women's Circles of which she had been a member. Grandmother Nuquist spoke all over the country on behalf of the Federation of Women's Clubs on issues of welfare and prison reform and child labor. My mother, representing the League of Women Voters or the NAACP, gave presentations about waste disposal or the need for fair housing in one forum or another, while my father was out several nights a week speaking about good government. When I was still a small child, Mother taught me the secrets of speech making. "Smile, speak slowly, keep your fingers moving along your notes so you don't lose your place, and look up often, especially to the back of the audience to make sure everyone can hear you." She insisted if I did that, no would notice how frightened I might be. I had many opportunities to test her theory over the years, giving little reports in church about the activities of Sunday School or our youth group, giving talks around Burlington about my summer in Luxembourg. I learned to disguise my nerves and speak my piece.

Mary McCarthy once said Vassar prepared women for a world that never was. For four years my fellow history majors and I had been encouraged to research an idea from all sides and to reach some conclusions about it, recognizing that new facts or knowledge would probably require its modification. We were taught to speak out and speak up, to listen, to argue and defend. We were not taught that once graduated and back in the world, there would be little interest in our carefully considered opinions or encouragement to express them.

By November of 1962 I had already relearned some caution. I was hired to type forty words per minute and run an adding machine at Pittsburgh Plate Glass. My ideas and opinions were beside the point. What was important to my job was that I learn to type an original and six carbon copies of a contract fast and accurately and to be efficient with the Dictaphone. That morning I mentioned to my boss, Mr. Smith, that I might be a few minutes late returning from lunch and would make up my time at the end of the day. I crept away from my desk just before noon. I didn't want Mr. Smith or my fellow secretaries to know I was going to speak at a Kiwanis meeting.

Now here I was, seated up on a dais at the head table next to the president. He introduced me very graciously, saying I had kindly agreed to be a substitute speaker on the subject of Cuba, filling in for my husband who had been called out of town at the last minute.

Hoping it would give me a little boost of confidence, I had dressed carefully for this talk. I wore my best dress, a black wool challis printed with huge white flowers, and the green jade earrings Arturo had given me to mark our engagement. I took a deep breath, projected a calm I didn't feel, and began. I told them I grew up in Vermont where Phil Hoff had just been elected the first Democrat governor in one hundred and eight years, and here I was in North Carolina where Terry Sanford, the newly elected Republican governor, had likewise broken a one-hundred-year tradition. The ice of habit was cracking everywhere.

Of course, I didn't mention the Civil War as being the event that had caused such hardened political affiliations. I believe I was, nevertheless, already a bit of a surprise to the assembled businessmen: a girl, a Yankee girl at that, a married Yankee girl, speaking to men, most of whom were old enough to be my father, about politics. Unsettling and unseemly.

I told them I was sorry Arturo couldn't be there. He was certainly more qualified to speak about the current situation in Cuba than I. However I had just devoted two years to a study of Cuban politics for the period from 1936 until the present. I had learned a great deal about the ruthless manipulation of Cuban government and business by the United States. I thought they might be interested in hearing an explanation, based in historical context, of why most Cubans had originally been so receptive to Fidel Castro and his appeal to nationalism and economic justice.

Arturo's parents had originally supported Castro and the overthrow of that corrupt and brutal dictator, Batista. They had been out in the streets when Castro entered Havana, cheering along with thousands of their fellow citizens. Now, however, with Castro's restriction of civil liberties and expropriation of private property, they fled to New York City, forced to abandon every possession except for one suitcase and a five-dollar bill. I then proceeded to put their story in a larger context.

My audience was certainly attentive, but whether they were interested in my account of our heavy hand in Cuban politics and business, or were simply amazed at my effrontery, I cannot say.

There were no follow-up invitations seeking my opinions on Cuba—or on any other topic, for that matter.

As much as I missed the world of ideas, I still did not give serious consideration to graduate school. Although I felt up to the task of giving speeches in High Point, I was unsure of my ability to meet the requirements of an advanced degree. Besides, I was a married woman. My responsibilities were to my husband, to help him advance in his career, to smooth his path. It was important to be noncontroversial, to provide background to his foreground. Graduate school was too assertive.

31 ❖ On the Fringe

Stroudsburg, Pennsylvania, 1968
High Point, North Carolina, 1963

Many people fear nothing more terribly than to take a position which stands out sharply and clearly from the prevailing opinion. The tendency of most is to adopt a view that is so ambiguous that it will include everything, and so popular, that it will include everybody. Not a few men who cherish lofty and noble ideals hide them under a bushel for fear of being called different.

—Martin Luther King, Jr.

Martin Luther King has been shot dead!

Betty's husband interrupted our League of Women Voters committee meeting to tell us. Shocked, I couldn't speak. A song began to loop in my brain. "Oh, no, it can't be so this morning. Oh, no, it can't be so this evening, so soon." The meeting continued, but I sat in my chair unable to hear what was being said. "Oh, no, it can't be so. Oh, no, it can't be so."

Home at last, I couldn't sleep. I paced our dark house, weeping in grief and frustration. Finally as it began to grow light, I put on a pot of coffee and turned on the television. A mezzo-soprano was singing, "Let us break bread together on our knees. Let us join hands together on our knees. When I fall on my knees with my face to the rising sun, O Lord, have mercy on me."

James Farmer appeared next. He was the director of CORE, the Congress of Racial Equality. "All civil rights leaders," he said, "live with the constant threat of assassination. To be effective, we have to decide that commitment to the cause is more important than fear of an early death. Dr. King made that commitment."

I was carried back to the church in the black section of High Point. It was an early evening in May 1963. Farmer had come to High Point to help the local members of CORE negotiate an end to the indignities of segregation. Restaurants, stores, bathrooms, water fountains, movies, schools, churches, and jobs were still segregated. The negotiations had not succeeded. This meeting had been called to organize a march, the next phase of protest.

Farmer was a commanding presence, large and elegantly suited. Speaking in burning, almost biblical, phrases, he told us it was time for justice. He told us we could achieve it by means of disciplined nonviolence. He appeared competent and unafraid.

By attending the meeting Arturo and I had violated the code. We had crossed the line from the paved, deliberately oblivious streets on the white side of town to the unpaved, unimproved, but rigorously taxed dirt roads on the black side. Despite James Farmer's reassuring presence, I was afraid. I never overcame my fears.

We came to the meeting at the invitation of Carol, Arturo's coworker at the studios where he designed make-believe rooms of furniture for photographic shoots. Carol's job was to make the beds, straighten pleats on bed skirts, stuff towels with tissue paper so they appeared plump and lush for the photographs, and fetch accessories from the storerooms. She was young, black, and, as Arturo had discovered in surreptitious conversations, angry. It was unusual for blacks and whites to work in such close proximity, but Carol's tasks were sufficiently close to housekeeping that no white worker wanted to perform them. At first Carol knew more about his job than Arturo did. He was grateful for her help and eager for her friendship. It was Carol who made my Cuban husband aware that there were lines dangerous to cross. They spoke in corners when no one else was around.

The first time we crossed the line was to have coffee and cake at Carol's home with her parents, some of her brothers and sisters, and her small daughter. Since we had not, after feckless hand-wringing about the lack of privacy in our apartment house, reciprocated the invitation, this rally was only our second clear violation.

During my last two years at Vassar, when CORE recruiters came looking for volunteers to ride on the freedom buses, I thought I wanted to join up. I convinced myself it was impossible because of financial considerations. I did not have the funds for transportation to the South. During summer vacations, I had to earn money to pay for my winter school expenses. I read the newspapers and knew about the violence the freedom riders encountered. I never admitted to myself that fear made my decision.

I don't believe a desire to ride the freedom buses ever crossed Arturo's mind. He simply considered the racial divide irrational and wrong.

For the first few months after coming to live in High Point, I managed to ignore the fact that I was accommodating myself to a system of apartheid. Race and civil rights were taboo topics of conversation in the white world where I lived. As a Yankee college girl who wore too much black, I was already a little suspect. Nevertheless, I was met with kind and friendly courtesy by my new acquaintances. I tried to be equally gracious to my coworkers at Pittsburgh Plate Glass, our neighbors in the Rowella Apartments, and Arturo's bosses at the design studio, who gave a small party in honor of the newlyweds. How could I respond to such kindness with rude inquiries about race relations? I was a newcomer. What did I really know about the lives and beliefs of these people?

I saw very few Negroes. There were the young boys who, during school hours, carried my groceries from the checkout counter to my car, despite my being taller and stronger than they were. There was my neighbor's elderly cleaning lady who slipped soundlessly past my screen door every day. Occasionally, through the swinging door of a restaurant kitchen, I saw black workers. Other than this nebulous contact, it was easy to avoid "the problem." I joined the choir of the Presbyterian Church across the street from our apartment house. That church was one of many in town where, shortly after this first CORE rally, Negroes attempting to attend a Sunday service were turned away at the door.

Carol's second invitation was a direct test of the sincerity of my (our) convictions. Did we really mean what we had been saying to each other and to her? Carol met us at the steps of the church. She was the church organist. Since she wouldn't be able to sit with us, she walked us inside and introduced us to the elderly pastor and his wife. They invited us to join them in their pew near the front of the church. Their welcome eased my initial acute discomfort, although I was embarrassed to receive what felt like special treatment. I thought we should be ignored, relegated to the back of the church, or not let in at all. Both grateful and ashamed, I was moved by their kindness.

The church was large. Attendance was sparse—people were scattered about the pews. I glanced around and saw that, in addition to Arturo and me, there was only one other white person in the sanctuary, a frail young man. We learned later that he was an organizer for CORE who had come down from Washington, D.C., with James Farmer.

Arturo and I were not the only ones who had to refer to the mimeographed sheets for the words to the songs Carol played on the organ: "We Shall Overcome," "Freedom," "Let Us Break Bread Together on Our Knees."

We were preparing to march to demand the right to be served in restaurants. Farmer began to train us in the philosophy and techniques of nonviolent protest. First we had to undergo self-purification. He harangued us on the importance of persistence, perseverance, and determination. He insisted that, despite injuries and setbacks, change would come. He warned that any of us who didn't feel able to endure suffering and still remain nonviolent would be kept from the march.

"You will learn not to fight back even when you are hit and spit upon."

We practiced kneeling down in such a way as to protect our heads, chests, and stomachs.

A series of meetings was held. Each night attendance increased. The training was repeated. The songs were sung again and again. Only two more whites appeared. They were from the North Carolina office of the American Friends Service Committee, the national service organization of the Quakers.

No one came from the local Quaker meeting. I was disappointed but not surprised. Old friends of my grandparents led its meetings for worship. They invited Arturo and me to tea after my arrival in High Point. That day I was shocked to discover blacks were not permitted inside their meeting house. I had heard all my life that Quakers opposed slavery. My great-great-great-grandfather Edgerton had left his prosperous farm in North Carolina, not far from High Point, for the unexplored wilds of the Northwest Territory, because the Quakers had said no person of conscience should live where men were held in bondage. Quakers believe each individual carries a spark of divine light. Quaker conscience and segregation could not coexist. I was profoundly disillusioned by their explanation that one had to accept local mores. I didn't argue with them, but I didn't pursue the relationship.

The night of the first march arrived. Arturo and I choked down a hasty supper. We were too nervous for much conversation. At the church we all practiced how to shield our bodies from rocks and beatings one more time. Farmer reminded us that it was to be a silent march. The collection plates were passed twice, once for money and once for knives, guns, chains, or any other weapons that people, despite the training, might have brought with them. Both times the plates filled. Even at that, some of the young men declared they could not march. They knew they would fight back if they were attacked. Others were ordered to stay out of the lines because the organizers doubted their commitment to nonviolence.

We were told where to assemble downtown. Arturo and I drove alone in our white Corvair and found a parking place on the route of the march near the assembly point. We couldn't get out of the car. For me it wasn't just physical fear—it was fear of being different, of somehow not appearing respectable to my handful of friendly new white acquaintances. But wasn't I protesting their ideas of respectability by attending these meetings?

Now the marchers passed by in silence. The line seemed so fragile, so small, so exposed. Still I stayed in my seat. Ashamed and sickened by my cowardice, I rolled down the window and spoke quiet words of support as the marchers passed by. At least, I thought, it offered a contrast to the jeers and taunts coming from High Point's white thugs, the establishment's tacit delegates. Carol passed, head high, apparently deaf to the obscenities and threats hurled her way.

After that first march, attendance at the nightly meetings increased dramatically. Soon the pews, the aisles, the vestibule, and even the outside steps were packed. The marches continued. Each night we attended the meeting, and then drove to the line, determined that tonight we would get out of the car. I waited for Arturo to open his door; he waited for me to open mine. It never happened.

Nothing about the marches appeared in the newspapers. Somehow word spread. The police did not appear. Considering what had occurred in other communities, this was perhaps a blessing. The marchers were left to face growing heckling and hostility alone. Tensions grew and "incidents" accumulated—beatings here, rocks thrown there.

At the boundary between the white and black sections of High Point, crowds of angry young whites and equally angry young black men confronted each other. Again there was no police presence.

It became increasingly risky to cross that divide after dark. We were objects of suspicion to both sides. Arturo drove as quickly as he could, looking straight ahead. I fought the temptation to duck beneath the level of the windshield, hoping naively that the presence of a woman in the car might keep the threat of attack down. It seemed to both of us that our white skins must be glowing in the glare of flashlights shown into our windows. We were amazed each time to find ourselves safe once again on the unlit dirt road that led to the rally and then back on the well-lit streets of white High Point at its conclusion.

Night after night the demonstrators walked in silence past the darkened stores, the movie theater, and the restaurants that excluded them. One night two hundred and fifty marchers were surrounded by a thousand screaming whites, brandishing baseball bats and throwing rocks and bottles. I prayed for the marchers not to stop, not to kneel down in defense. I was afraid the mob would overwhelm them. The demonstrators never paused. Once more Carol passed by, this time holding the hand of her six-year-old daughter. Still we sat in the car.

Now the young organizer, a marked man because of his participation in the demonstrations, decided it was time to return to Washington. He didn't want to put any black at further risk that night by driving downtown to the bus station. We drove him, glad to finally take some action, no matter how small. He crouched down on the floor behind the front seat. We threw a blanket over him. Arturo drove around the block by the station until the bus was ready to depart. At the last second, we slowed, our passenger threw off the blanket, leaped from the car, dashed up the stairs of the bus, and made it safely out of town. We drove carefully home, watching over our shoulders to make sure we weren't being followed.

The next day for the first time, the newspaper did carry the story that a white mob had attacked marchers. It printed a few graphic photographs taken at the scene. However, back in the white world where I spent my days, no one mentioned the article. I, too, said nothing, as I had said nothing for the previous weeks. I went about the office, spoke to my next-door neighbor, bought my groceries, and acted as though I had nothing more planned for my evening than dinner and a book. I felt like a spy, a member of the underground. I never discussed what I was doing with anyone. In fact, I lived in dread that someone would find out. Arturo talked about the demonstrations at work, in whispers, with people who were participating in them, but never with any white coworker.

Each evening as we ate our hurried supper, we agreed we would march this time, but we never joined as the line formed after the rally at the church. Now at last the demonstrations had become news. Photographers from the local paper and nearby TV stations came to the church every night. Their lights swept over us. I tried to appear confident, although I was in fact so apprehensive I could hardly breathe.

Thugs had failed to take care of the situation. This time the demand for justice wasn't going to go away. The city fathers were forced to negotiate. CORE agreed to a two-week suspension of further demonstrations if the mayor would immediately appoint a bi-racial committee. The committee was to find the means to implement an end to segregation. Mr. Farmer had departed, his job done. Mrs. D. Z. Mitchell, CORE's local chairperson, and John Langford, its local attorney, now led the negotiations. The Sunday, June 9, 1963, edition of the *High Point Enterprise* reported:

> Members of the committee have reportedly conferred almost daily … on grievances of the Negro populace. They have formed into subcommittees to carry out the assignment from the City Council to work for integration on a 'reasonable' timetable.
>
> Emphasis has reportedly been placed on integrating local restaurants, motels and hotels and theaters—described by Negro members of the committee as 'sore spots' of discrimination. Conferences have been held with operators of some High Point businesses.
>
> Four Negroes are serving on the 12-member committee. Langford is a member.

The newspaper printed an article about the June 11 open hearing conducted by the Bi-Racial Committee in the City-County Building to obtain material for its report. Two hundred and fifty people crowded the room, the great majority of whom were black. Many rose to speak out for desegregation. "We don't want to bother you white people, we don't want you to bother us. We just want to come and go as we please and spend our money where we want to spend it." T.R. McRae said, "I am proud to be a Negro. I am a Negro with honesty and dignity. I have been in High Point for twenty-eight years and I am a respectable citizen — if I have to say so myself — and when I walk down the street I feel as good as the mayor." Having fought for his country, he was "not proud that Negroes in America have to be discriminated against because their skin is pigmented... what have you [white men] lost if you stop discriminating? Democracy is as free as the wind and there is enough for all of us."

Not one white minister attended, nor did any representatives from white business or community organizations. One white schoolteacher, Miss Genevieve Moore, told the crowd that packed the municipal courtroom, "We will all get used to each other. As we begin doing things together we will become accustomed to associating with people of different races." B.T. Bell, the representative from the American Friends Service Committee who had marched each evening, rose in support of integration. Otherwise, the whites who spoke wanted things to remain as they had always been. "The Good Lord said to us in the New Testament each of us has a place and each must keep that place." "Is there a statute on the books which will permit any man to demand that he be permitted to go to a man's restaurant?" "God made man in five colors ... and He put each where He wanted them to be."

That night both Arturo and I finally declared ourselves. Because we were white, we couldn't keep silent without appearing to agree with what the whites around us were saying. Trembling, I got up to speak my little piece. "I believe one of the most basic American principles is that of 'liberty and justice for all.' Until we extend this to all our citizens, then this is not the America we pledge allegiance to in the pledge to the flag." Arturo rose and gave a somewhat lengthy testimony. His main point was that he had been proud to become an American citizen in 1958 and to pledge his allegiance to the United

States. By supporting the movement to end segregation, in his opinion he was fulfilling part of that pledge.

However, the strain of standing up at last was apparently too much for us. The following week we went to New York City on vacation. We began looking for jobs. We convinced ourselves that life in High Point was impossible. I was too far from home. We both missed New York. In New York we could have friends on the basis of mutual interests without regard to race.

So in July we left High Point and moved to an air-conditioned apartment in New York's Murray Hill. There we were surrounded by friends who shared our opinions about liberty and justice. We told our High Point story over and over.

That winter I was stunned to read in the *New York Times* that one of my classmates, a black woman from Cincinnati, had gone to Alabama to work for civil rights and was now in prison there. I wanted to write to her, but I felt so guilty about my lack of courage and its stark contrast to her bravery that I couldn't think quite what I would say.

32 ❖ The American Field Service

New York City, 1963–1965

Before our precipitous flight from North Carolina, Arturo and I both obtained jobs in New York. Arturo went to work doing window and floor displays for W. & J. Sloane, a furniture store on Fifth Avenue, for one hundred dollars a week. I found a job with the American Field Service in their beautiful new building at 313 East 43rd Street, just at the edge of Tudor City and only a long block from United Nations headquarters. My beginning salary was sixty-five dollars a week. I was ready for a fresh start, although sexual frustration was still a major, if unspoken, problem, at least for me.

The Pleasures of Landscape

This morning air:
The friend who didn't move to a different town
The mother with no expectations
The delicate touch of the other lover, the one I
    never had
As always, this air touched my skin,
the backs of my knees, the flesh
above my elbow, my hands.
It was easier to love the air
than it was to love you.
This air gave itself endlessly.

Our apartment building on East 35th Street had twenty-four-hour doormen, polished floors, and an elevator. The rent was only $165 a month, which exactly met the guideline I read in a woman's magazine of twenty-five percent of our income. It was within easy walking distance of both our jobs.

Carnivorous

A man stopped me on the street,
invited me to go away with him
although I don't think he meant
forever. But since I was on my way
to meet Arturo, I turned him down.
I wanted to go with the man.
He didn't seem dangerous.
I could sizzle up at the slightest hint
of heat—a brush of shoulder
against shoulder, a glance, a voice,
a smile. Though still firm, I was
already well-marbled. It could have been
some banquet.

I made it safely to my new desk. My college roommate Caro and another good friend from Vassar, Adele, had been employed at AFS for the year since our graduation. A notice had appeared on the bulletin board outside the Vassar placement office that AFS was seeking job applicants. At the time I was interested because of my former happy time in the AFS Americans Abroad Summer Program, but Arturo and I would not be living in New York. So I recommended the job to my friends.

But now in the summer of 1963 I was hired as a correspondent. My responsibility was for a section of Southern California. At least once a month I wrote a personal letter to each of the students we had placed in families there, and the students were required to reply with a monthly letter of their own. The theory was that a student unhappy in his or her home or school would convert that unhappiness to a generally unfavorable view of the United States and would carry that negative view home. We were to ferret out any problems, to know each student well enough to tease out difficulties that, for whatever reason, they were otherwise reluctant to reveal.

Our modest goal was to foster world friendship and understanding according to the AFS motto: "Walk together, talk together, all ye peoples of the earth. Then and only then shall ye have peace." At the time AFS still received substantial funding from the State Department.

The program had positive propaganda value, but only if the students had a good time. So AFS gave careful individual attention to each student.

My desk overlooking 43rd Street was one of many grouped in a large open room on the second floor of the AFS building. Our leader, Steven Galatti, sat behind a waist-high dividing wall on the opposite side of the room. A round toad of a man, he appeared not to sit at his desk but rather to squat behind it, overflowing his chair. Constant smoke from the cigarette dangling from his mouth obscured hooded eyes and an assortment of warts and moles on his pouchy dark face. Ash, some still smoldering, some turned to gray dust, spilled from an overflowing ashtray across a six-inch layer of papers stacked in untidy piles or falling out of manila folders that completely obscured the surface of his desk.

Mr. Galatti's association with the American Field Service dated back to its founding during World War I. Before the United States entered the war, young Americans living in France had wanted to do something useful. They began AFS as an ambulance service, driving wounded soldiers away from the front. Mr. Galatti had been one of those drivers.

The ambulance service had been reactivated during World War II under Mr. Galatti's leadership. He remained in New York throughout the war, directing operations from the AFS office, then located on Beaver Street. Mr. Galatti did his work for AFS from 3:00 P.M. until late at night, after he had completed his regular day at a brokerage firm. Until 1954 Mr. Galatti remained an unpaid volunteer.

There was some money left in the accounts of the ambulance service at the end of the war. Mr. Galatti's vision and that of others among the drivers was to put those funds to use to foster better understanding between the young people of the world. He thought if individual young people came to know one another, they would be less willing to go to war when they grew up.

In 1947 fifty-two students came from eleven countries to spend a year living with American families and attending school. By 1963 more than two thousand students from fifty countries were arriving in the U.S., while many young Americans were spending a summer abroad.

Mr. Galatti opposed hierarchy as a matter of principle and would have nothing to do with the trappings of power. He hunched at his desk with no office walls or formidable secretary to defend him. Any of us could approach him at any time. We knew, however, or soon learned, that the problem we brought to him had better be a major one, something that couldn't be solved by anyone in the office other than himself. A few pointed questions from Mr. Galatti and the neophyte scurried away, red-faced, to do the research or to ask the person she or he should have asked in the first place.

Caro and Adele and I were among the early personnel to be interviewed and hired as paid employees. For years much of the work was done by volunteers and ex-ambulance drivers. Although only a few volunteers still held full-time positions in 1963, many came by to help at peak periods or just to visit.

Often they brought along a cake or cookies or a big platter of cheese and crackers. Every week or so, Mr. Galatti would rise up and bellow, "Goodies!" We would make our way to his desk. There we would help ourselves to the "goody" balanced precariously atop the cascading piles of paper, cookie crumbs or bits of cheese scattering into the general disarray.

When Mr. Galatti spoke, the toad turned into a prince of humor and grace. He was a man of charm and enormous personal force. We adored him. We worked hard for him.

In addition to writing to my students and trying to resolve any problems their replies revealed, my job included meeting the ships and airplanes of arriving students, making them feel welcome and cared for, and checking their documents to be sure all were in order. I also read the application forms of students and potential host families and helped to find good matches among them.

For much of my first week at the AFS office in July of 1963, most of the desks around me were empty. The staff was in Washington chaperoning the students gathered there from all over the country, as they were every year at the end of their stay, to see the sights and to be received by the president. I regretted that my job had not begun in time for me to see President Kennedy. I was an ardent supporter, although I had been too young to cast a vote for him. Arturo and I had driven to Washington from High Point ostensibly to see the

Mona Lisa there on temporary exhibit, but what had compelled both of us was the excitement generated in Washington by the presence of John and Jackie Kennedy. The glamorous Jackie, after all, had attended Vassar.

I consoled myself with the thought I would surely have the opportunity to see President Kennedy in 1964.

Within a month after my arrival at AFS, the clerks working in the file room began to talk about a civil rights demonstration that was to take place on August 28th in Washington. The people working in the large open office area, primarily young women, were, with only two exceptions, white. The clerks and the postal room employees were black. While they obtained permission to take a day off to attend, I was too timid to ask for a day off so soon after beginning my job. Consequently I missed one of the bright shining moments of the twentieth century, the March on Washington and Martin Luther King, Jr.'s "I Have a Dream" speech.

From the very first I loved my job. I felt I was doing something that mattered. My fellow workers were for the most part congenial. My boss in D Division, Alice Gerlach, had been one of my chaperones on the ship the *Arosa Kulm* in 1957. Continuously overworked, she could be gruff and abrupt, but she was also fair and efficient, and we got on very well.

The students, from all over the world, were wonderfully bright and attractive. As they passed through New York some of them, for one reason or another, would spend a day or two in the dormitory on the third floor. To keep them occupied in the evening we organized impromptu talent shows. There might be performances by a dancer from Ethiopia, a guitarist from Brazil, and a Norwegian folk singer all wearing traditional costumes. Sitting in the darkened first-floor lounge watching and listening, it seemed to me the benefits of peace and friendship would inevitably become apparent to all.

On November 22, 1963, I was writing a letter at my desk, glancing idly from time to time at the men across the street at work building the new Ford Foundation headquarters. They were close enough to catch my eye and one would occasionally wave or blow a kiss.

Suddenly from behind me a voice shouted, "President Kennedy has been shot! It's on the television!"

Most of us rose from our desks and ran down the flight of stairs to the lounge. There we stood in stunned silence, watching the confusion on the screen, hearing the contradictory reports about the president's condition. Finally, just after 1:00 p.m., the official announcement was made. President Kennedy was dead. In a strange state of shock, I made my way back to my desk, thinking for some reason that I should return to work.

Through the window came the sound of a whistle. I watched the men across the street gather in a half-circle in front of the foreman. I could see he was talking to them and knew he must be telling them that the president had been murdered. One by one the men removed their yellow hard hats, held them across their burly chests, and bowed their heads. A few of them knelt down in the clutter and mess of construction. My shock lifted and I began to weep. Through my tears I watched the men gather up their lunch buckets and quietly walk away.

Without speaking to anyone I put my papers in a drawer, left the building and walked home. That day I experienced for the first time a moment that would consciously and permanently divide my life. There was the world before President Kennedy was shot, and there was the world that followed. I couldn't have imagined then that it was just the beginning of horror upon horror, and that finally I would become almost numb to public tragedy.

But in the meantime life continued. I was promoted to area supervisor and my salary increased to eighty-five dollars a week. In February 1964 I was sent west to visit students, their host families, and the local AFS volunteer organizations that raised money, found families, and were responsible for the day-to-day management of the program in their communities.

Howling winds and blizzards accompanied me as I flew from Denver to Cheyenne and then to Great Falls, Montana. It was forty degrees below zero when I arrived in Missoula, Montana. I had splurged on a chestnut-brown coat at the January sales at Bonwit's and had purchased a long brown, green, and white plaid mohair scarf to go with it. Even my new finery failed to keep me warm on that frigid trip.

From Missoula I continued on to Spokane, Twin Falls, Salt Lake City, and finally, after three-and-a-half weeks, home to New York. Twenty-three years old and counseling students, meeting with families, giving little speeches in high school auditoriums and community centers, and writing reports in my motel rooms at night, I thought I was hot stuff.

Life in New York was certainly an improvement over life in High Point. Satisfaction came from my work and my friends. I joined St. George's Choral Society and was asked to be part of its chamber group. But almost every night that I managed to get home before 7:30, Arturo wanted to go out somewhere. I would fix a quick supper and then we would set off. If we were going anyplace in midtown, Arturo insisted that we walk to save bus or subway fare.

Tickets to the top tier of Balanchine's New York City Ballet in its new home at Lincoln Center cost $1.05 each. We sat in the single file of seats high above the stage. We attended each change in program. In summer we went to all the free concerts and plays presented in Central Park.

At that time there were still movie theaters on 42nd Street. They were dirty and dilapidated, but not yet exclusively devoted to porn. These theaters featured reruns at much reduced prices. Their clientele consisted mainly of drunks and addicts, shabby disheveled people looking for an inexpensive place out of the weather to spend their days and nights. The theaters smelled terrible, and stale cigarette smoke and alcohol mingled with other unidentifiable but definitely unsavory odors. The seats were torn and stained.

I hated going to these theaters. If we couldn't afford tickets to a real movie, I preferred to stay at home. I longed to stay at home anyway, finding myself increasingly fatigued by the unending pace. Arturo let me know I was selfish and inconsiderate of his wishes and a snob for objecting to the 42nd Street theaters. So, night after night, off we trudged.

There were very few other women, especially young women, in attendance. Occasionally, to my mortification, the pathetic old geezer in the seat next to me would press his leg against mine, or rub my thigh, or even begin to masturbate. Too polite to hit the man or to scream, my solution was to change to another seat. Arturo, engrossed in the movie, had to be persuaded to move. His way of dealing with trouble was to turn deaf and dumb to it, to pretend it didn't exist. The old guy wasn't bothering *him*, after all.

One night a man and woman slid in past us after we were seated, Arturo on the aisle and me beside him. Suddenly the man slumped in my direction. His companion stood up, forced herself past his limp body, and disappeared up the aisle. Arturo ignored the interruption and continued to watch the movie. Horrified and frightened, I pushed the man away from me. He sagged forward out of his seat, his head propped against the seat in front of him. I was sure he was dead. After some minutes of my insistent whispering, Arturo went up the aisle to notify the usher. The man beside me never stirred.

Shaken, I wanted to leave, but Arturo wanted to see the end of the movie. We moved across the aisle. While paramedics rolled a stretcher down the aisle and removed the body I sat beside Arturo, overcome with frustration and fury. Disappointment with my husband solidified that night. I could force it to the back of my mind for longer or shorter periods of time, but it never went away. I had assumed the bargain for my acquiescence was that he would act on my behalf when necessary. Instead, he proved to be more inert than I was. If I ever needed him, I could be sure he wouldn't be there. We were both waiting for a mother-in-charge to take over, as had been the pattern of our respective youths, but neither of us was prepared to assume such a role.

My mother always told me my life was undeservedly easy. To her I appeared to slide through without problems or complications. I got what I wanted—a trip to Europe, a college scholarship, friends. About this time she came to New York for a short visit. One morning over a cup of instant coffee at the small round table in our apartment, apropos of nothing in particular, she said she guessed even I wasn't going to escape. Life was going to catch up with me after all. I assumed she was speaking about my marriage. I hadn't said anything to her. I thought I had successfully concealed my problems, as I had always done. She had always wanted to hear about my successes, not my difficulties. She proved to be more observant than I realized although I denied, of course, that anything was wrong and quickly changed the subject.

In July of 1964 I did go to Washington as a chaperone for the end-of-year stay. It was exciting to be invited to a reception on the White House lawn, although our host was only President Johnson. An appointment with the president, however much *I* might think

Lyndon Johnson was a stand-in for John Kennedy, the *real* president, nevertheless required the guests to be on time.

Police cars with screaming sirens and flashing lights led our procession of forty buses. Once underway, we never paused. Police stationed at every intersection stopped all traffic until our last bus had passed. In my bus at the head of the line, we all sang melancholy renditions of songs of the day as we pulled up to park beside the White House fence: " The answer, my friend, is blowing in the wind." President Kennedy dominated my thoughts as we were hurried through a gate to chairs set up before a temporary stage on the lawn.

We perked up when a military band began to play "Hail to the Chief." We all stood while the president strode briskly onto the stage to polite applause. Then his young daughters, Lynda Bird and Lucy, came out, their hair piled in lacquered beehives, their dresses short and bright. As our boys began to cheer and whistle, it occurred to me that we had failed to instruct them in the finer points of protocol. They had assumed the general informality of American life extended to every occasion. At last by much furtive shushing and many dirty looks, we got them quieted down. I don't remember a word of the president's short speech. Afterwards we climbed back aboard and were carried busload by busload to the families throughout the region that were hosting us for our stay.

Sadly, Mr. Galatti died that summer. We continued on as before but everyone knew AFS would be a different organization without his leadership.

Arturo was soon dissatisfied with his job at W. & J. Sloane. His future there did seem to be limited. We were getting by on our respective salaries, but certainly not getting ahead. Should I become pregnant, there was no realistic way we could live in New York on only his salary.

So he began a job search that resulted in an offer from a company in Stroudsburg, Pennsylvania, that made display cases for department stores. Arturo would design customized cases and the interiors of the stores into which they would be placed. The offer was generous, more than doubling his salary, and included frequent weekend access to a company suite in the Warwick Hotel on Sixth Avenue. He accepted the offer.

AFS was as reluctant to accept my resignation as I was to give it. In an attempt to keep me, they offered to pay for my commute and to make whatever schedule changes might therefore be required. A daily bus ride from Stroudsburg would have been an impossible grind. If we had moved to New Jersey, halfway between our respective jobs, it might have worked. The idea, however, never crossed my mind.

I thought then that I was stuck for life. I had made my bed, lonely as it might be. My real job was to be an emotional support for my husband, to be a credit to him, to make a comfortable home and life wherever he might take me. So I had been raised and so I still believed.

For the few years we were in Stroudsburg, I became my mother. I did secretarial work part-time for Arturo's company. And, of course, I continued to sing as choir member and soloist in the local Methodist church. I joined the League of Women Voters and was soon devoting more than twenty hours a week to its various study groups and committees. One time after I had given a community presentation, Arturo's annoyed boss remarked, "Your wife certainly likes to get her name in the paper. What can she possibly know about U.S.-China relations? She's too young to know anything!"

There was some truth to that. I knew more about U.S.-China relations than I did about my own with Arturo. There would be times when I thought everything would work out, followed by long periods of despair. Arturo and I were polite to each other, but our conversations were about everything except our increasingly distant relationship. We never spoke of our feelings.

We wanted to have a child, the next thing on our agenda. Arturo earned more than enough to support a child. After we had made the decision, for the brief time before I became pregnant, sex was relatively unproblematic, frequent, and almost enthusiastic.

33 ❖ Labor Intensive

Stroudsburg, March 10, 1966

Our first baby due in May, I carried two heavy bags of groceries home from the store in Stroudsburg. I hoped Arturo would say "Oh, that's too heavy for you." He didn't.

That night I developed what I was sure were contractions, regular and increasingly strong. I phoned the doctor, who advised us to go immediately to the hospital. There I was led to a labor room and told to undress and put on a gown. My vital signs were checked, my contractions timed. The nurse left me to labor on my own. Perhaps it was assumed the laborers would be too busy to notice that the room was as drab and bare as a prison cell, with a metal bed and bare beige walls. Nothing of beauty, nothing to distract my attention. No one allowed in, Arturo remained in the waiting room. I heard disconcerting noises — exclamations, groans, screams. The nurse came in every once in a while to see if I was making progress. The contractions continued, two minutes apart, painful, but I was resolved to make no sound. A raised voice seemed so lacking in dignity, unladylike. I had certainly never heard my mother raise hers.

The doctor hoped the contractions would stop since two months remained to reach full term. They didn't. In the morning he arrived. After examining me he said the baby would have to be delivered, since a little drainage of amniotic fluid suggested there was now an opening for infection. He would let things continue naturally for twenty-four more hours and then make a decision on the best way to proceed. Meanwhile I might as well be more comfortable in a regular postpartum room. He thought I would continue in my present condition of steady but nonproductive contractions.

The transfer complete, Arturo was allowed in to see me. I told him he might as well go home. He did.

In the meantime the contractions continued. The pain was intense. I thought my back was going to burst, but I didn't yell. It was difficult to make polite conversation with the woman in the next bed and to exclaim over the wonder of her brand-new baby. I managed.

The pink lady wheeled in her cart. I gasped that I didn't need any crackers or magazines, thank you very much.

The nurse had apparently not received information from the doctor as to what I was doing on her ward and decided I just wanted attention. I rang the bell to let her know the contractions were now one-and-a-half minutes apart. She ordered me to calm down and refused to examine me.

She appeared with a lunch tray and insisted I eat. Between contractions I pushed things around on the plate to make it look like I was following her orders. I managed to swallow a couple of spoonfuls of applesauce.

Then a warm gush of water flooded the bed. I rang the bell again. Again the nurse reprimanded me, wouldn't come close enough to look even when I lifted the covers, and told me I was being ridiculous. I tried to explain there was only some leakage before. She wouldn't hear me. If I didn't settle down she'd have to call the doctor to get something for my unsettled nerves. Oh, I hoped she would. He would understand. He would believe me.

Next I was helplessly groaning and pushing. She happened in the room and told me to stop. "I can't." At last she looked. The baby had crowned.

Somehow she wrestled me into a wheelchair and rushed me down the hall to the delivery room, yelling out to the nurse at the desk to call the doctor. I tried to sit at an angle in hope that I wouldn't crush my baby.

The doctor soon arrived, laughed to the attendants that he had just had his suit dry-cleaned and now he'd have to do it again—no time to suit up. He told me that since I had eaten there couldn't be any anesthesia. That was fine with me. It seemed a little beside the point by now. He inserted forceps and pulled out Omar, all four pounds, twelve ounces of him and who, within a day, developed an infection, no doubt as a result of the unsterile condition of his birth.

The good old days.

They wheeled me back to my room. Nurse Nemesis told me I was very brave. I told her I was glad I was not crazy after all. I telephoned Arturo's office to let him know he was a father.

I should have screamed like a banshee. Being a "lady," not raising my voice, could have cost me my son. I needed to learn to raise my voice!

After a scary few weeks Omar began to gain weight and the jaundice faded, along with my fear that he would die.

From the day he was born I was passionately in love with my son, and Arturo was proud to have made one and to have something so very fine to show to the world. Omar took up a lot of what had been the lonely space in our lives.

When he was still a very young baby, we began to take him to the suite in the Warwick for weekends. Pushing his perambulator through Central Park, we looked perfect—a beautiful baby, fortunate to have such attractive, prosperous-appearing parents. Sometimes I thought this *appearance* was Arturo's true ambition, as much as he could hope for, sufficient to his needs.

34 ❖ The Crash

After only two years, once again Arturo was dissatisfied with his job. He quit to open a private design business with another man from the firm. They printed up professional-looking cards and brochures and made many calls but failed to attract clients. Arturo thought we should move to Allentown, a larger city that might offer more opportunity.

I had made good friends in Stroudsburg, first through my participation in the League of Women Voters, and then among the people I had met in other civic organizations and from my singing. I did not want to leave, but I realized it was an economic necessity.

In Allentown we rented a dark, unattractive little row house on a side street. The rent was low enough we thought we could manage. Arturo pursued various ideas without notable success, and money remained extremely scarce. We had moved from a comfortable position in a small community to obscurity, poverty, and insecurity. I hid my resentment.

When Omar was two we put him into a day-care program, still an unusual concept in the late sixties, run by the Volunteers of America. I took a job in the business office of a private girls' school. I was very unhappy about the long daily separation from my son, and, although VOA provided excellent care, it rankled me to have consigned Omar to a charitable organization.

Grandmother Nuquist died in Osceola in 1968, and my father gave us enough of his inheritance that we could make a down payment on a wonderful forty-year-old duplex near the center of Allentown.

Then, on Jan. 2, 1969, we were returning from a Christmas visit to Vermont. It had snowed heavily the day before and numerous icy patches remained on the New York State Thruway. The temperature was just above zero. Omar was in the back seat dressed in his puffy snowsuit, wrapped in blankets, and surrounded by the extra pillows we had taken with us to Burlington.

Arturo complained of fatigue and asked me to drive. When I took over the wheel, the car felt strange and hard to control. "There's something wrong. Don't you think we had better stop and have it checked over?"

Arturo insisted everything was fine; it was just the weather or the road surface. I thought it must surely be more than that. Something *was* wrong. I felt it. Arturo immediately went to sleep. I wondered if his fatigue was caused by the difficulty of driving a defectively operating car. As was increasingly the case, anger swept over me, but I drove on, struggling to keep the car straight in the lane.

Suddenly I was fishtailing wildly back and forth across two lanes and into the median. In absolute terror, I felt the car begin to roll over. Then I was coming up out of blank space. My son was crying, "Mama, I want to get out de car! Mama, I want to get out de car! Mama!"

I turned toward Arturo, but no one was there. Only an empty seat and an open door. I had killed my husband! I couldn't let Omar see whatever horror was outside there somewhere. Despite the urgency of his voice, I tried to speak calmly, "Wait just a minute, honey. I'll get you out in a minute. Stay here now."

I struggled out from beneath the steering wheel. My door was also open. I had to find Arturo. I had been thinking bad thoughts about him and now I had killed him. Fighting to remain conscious, I felt as though I were looking down a long dark tunnel. My head spinning, I staggered across the snow to a still form lying on the ground. Arturo.

I lay down beside him. I was dimly aware other people were gathering around us.

"Please," I say. "Please get my son. He's in the car."

A voice told me they had him. "He's fine. Don't worry, he's fine."

Another voice said "Just lie still. Don't try to move."

I forced myself to ask the unbearable question. "Is my husband alive?"

"Yes," the voice said, "He's alive."

Then a woman's voice was whispering in my ear. "Don't worry," it said, "my husband is a doctor. He'll help your husband. He'll be all right. You'll be all right. I'm a nurse, you see. I know. Just be still now."

"Thank you" I said. "Thank you, thank you." I asked her what her name was, but she just repeated that I shouldn't worry.

An ambulance arrived. Arturo was lifted onto a stretcher. They came to help me up, but I discovered I was unable to raise my body. There was excruciating pain in my back and neck. They put stabilizers around me and lifted me on to a stretcher, too. Omar rode in the ambulance with us to the hospital. He was very quiet.

Arturo and I spent the rest of the day in adjoining cubicles in Albany Medical Center's emergency room. Arturo regained consciousness in the ambulance, but he remained groggy and confused. We each had a series of x-rays. In addition to Arturo's concussion, the ankle of his bad leg was broken. A doctor informed me that Arturo's other leg had suffered a terrible laceration, a foot-long gash that revealed both bone and the nerve. Miraculously, the nerve was intact. The doctor told me that nine times out of ten when a leg is caught on the knife edge at the bottom of unpadded dashboards the way Arturo's was, it is cut right off.

My right ear was shredded. I had compression fractures of the fifth and sixth cervical vertebrae and some nerve damage, a combination of numbness and pain, in the center of my back, but I was not paralyzed. Omar was unhurt except for a cut on one finger. I was aware of our amazing good fortune.

The state police came to speak with me. Our two rear tires were worn completely bald. Apparently they had blown and the police surmised the blowout caused me to lose control of the car. Didn't I know it was dangerous to drive on tires like that? I don't admit that it had not occurred to me that tires wear out. My father had always taken care of such matters, and I had never driven until after I was married. They, too, told me we were lucky to be alive. According to witnesses the car rolled over numerous times before landing upright.

Meanwhile Omar was roaming the emergency room. Not yet three, he was crawling under the curtains that separate the cubicles and running up and down the center aisle. A man was brought in screaming. His stomach was pumped free of poison while Omar watched the gruesome spectacle. He watched Arturo's leg being stitched back together. He saw the repeated siphoning of blood from my ear. Through it all he didn't cry.

As the hours wore on, I heard the frustrated exclamations of the doctors. "Can't you keep that kid out of here?" "Hey, don't touch that." "Leave that alone!" I was aware that the nurses were doing their best to be kind, but they were too busy for much more than a pat on the head or a friendly smile. One of them took him to the cafeteria for a dinner-time hamburger, for which I was deeply grateful.

In the evening a woman from social services came to tell me they had found a foster home for Omar. I was devastated by the thought that he would go with strangers, people I knew nothing about, on top of everything else he had experienced on this day. I remembered that a family we knew from Stroudsburg had recently moved to the Albany area. I pleaded with the woman to contact them and ask if they could keep Omar for a few days. Just before Arturo and I were transferred to our room, they came to pick up Omar. It was very hard to say goodbye. He seemed to accept the separation. I hoped he understood it wasn't forever.

For the next four days Arturo and I were incognito. Neither of us could move. There was no phone in the room. Inexplicably the nurses said they couldn't make a call for us. Finally I thought to demand to see the social service worker again. No one knew where we were. I was supposed to have been at work three days ago. I had no idea how my son was. Would she please call my parents to let them know what had happened to us.

She made the call. My mother was ill with cancer and the chemotherapy she was undergoing to fight it but, nevertheless, my parents drove to Albany and took Omar back to Burlington with them. At the request of the state police, the family who had kept Omar had removed our possessions from the car. They told my parents not to go see it. It would only upset them. It was hard to believe any of us survived.

Arturo and I spent twenty-one days in the hospital. At last my parents brought Omar back to us. A friend from Stroudsburg, a physician, drove up to take the three of us to her home. We remained a week and then, supplied with groceries and other necessities, returned to Allentown.

We spent another week recuperating. I made arrangements to be picked up by the van that took girls to the school so, despite a back brace and fierce pain, I could return to work. Arturo watched Omar at home as well as he was able. For months we lived on my check and our insurance. We had received payments from both our medical and our car insurance policies, which was perfectly legal according to an accountant we called.

One morning I was awakened by the loud falling call, *phew, phew, phew,* of a cardinal searching for a mate. Raising the shade, I looked out the window to see him sitting in glorious red splendor on the telephone wire just outside the bedroom. For the first time in many months I was aware of beauty, of something outside the painful struggle to make it through each day. I took it as a sign of hope. I realized I would recover; Arturo was recovering; alone or together, we would be relatively whole and strong again.

In the fall of 1969 I began a graduate program in social relations, a combination of sociology, cultural anthropology, and social psychology at Lehigh University, then still a male school at the undergraduate level. I hoped that graduate school would help improve my diminishing feelings of self-worth and eventually make me eligible for challenging work. Arturo abandoned the idea of an independent design firm and took a job as a designer for a furniture store.

Between Arturo's salary and my stipend as a graduate assistant, we were able to pay the bills. Omar remained in day-care.

That fall the department chairman went to a conference and asked me to deliver for him his lecture on marital adjustment. The text made me so angry that I argued against its thesis — it should not be the wife's responsibility to accommodate, smooth over, and make the adjustments so life would be easy for her man. The husband and the wife should be equally responsible. I got a standing ovation from the male audience, more from my energy and vehemence than from my argument, I imagine, but I was beginning to wake up. I taught a course called Social Problems and deviated from the text there, too. The war in Vietnam wasn't part of the curriculum until I included it.

On November 15, 1969, I traveled on one of the buses going from the Lehigh Valley to Washington, D.C., to the massive antiwar demonstration. I arrived to sit among the huge crowd gathered peacefully on the Mall listening to speeches and songs, a little shaken by my walk past tanks with their long guns pointing at me, ranks of soldiers massed against me, and the faint smell of what I assumed to be teargas. I took this show of force quite personally, being sure I had the right to protest peacefully against an unnecessary war.

In March of 1970 Mother was close to death from pancreatic cancer after a fierce three-year fight. I took leave to go home to be with her.

Mother

Father had done the best
he could do, put up a card table
in the guest room beside her bed,
leased a telephone
for thirty days, and put it there
for her, but the room looked sparse,
temporary, and she a stranger to it.
She's not eating, he told me,
she hardly sleeps.
He was bewildered
that after all these years
she should want to sleep alone.
I went to work. Every meal
I set the tray with her polished silver,
roses in the white jade vase,
crisp embroidered napkins
from the camphorwood chest.
She ate perfect poached eggs,
salmon mousse, sugar cookies,
the edges an even brown,
applesauce made with the skins
but milled smooth. She could pretend
I was what she wanted. I knew
all her recipes for a graceful life.
For a few days, they eased us both.

Candidate

Mother and I spoke final good-byes
in her bedroom, she insisting I go,
there was nothing to be gained,
nothing more could be done.
She whispered she wanted to hear
my voice one more time,

so when the taxi came I managed
to call out something, I don't know what,
but not the words burning the back
of my throat—please, I can't leave,
let me stay.

Holding my son's hand, I crossed the frozen
boards of the porch, the snow-banked path
to the taxi's engulfing heat, was patient
with his happy chatter, made sure not
to worry him with tears, helped him up
the stairs of the airplane, forced a smile
to the attendant, polite about the mist
of white grief overtaking me.

Arturo thought it a fine photo opportunity,
his son's first plane ride. He met us with a camera.
On the steps, a young woman dressed for winter,
returning from this final visit. I held my son's hand
and, even then, as expected, smiled and waved.

We drove back for the funeral, of course. Arturo told me not to cry. I didn't, but I was inwardly consumed by grief. I managed to muddle through my teaching responsibilities but was accumulating incompletes in my coursework.

Then, on May 4, 1970, at Kent State University four students were shot dead by the Ohio National Guard and nine more were wounded. Some had been protesting our invasion of Cambodia announced by President Nixon on April 30th; some had simply been walking by. Lehigh students, previously mostly nonpolitical, erupted in protest. They joined four million other college students across the country in strike. Although their grievances and demands were somewhat muddled—inclusion in university governance, protest against the war, fury with what they saw as bad decisions by those in power—their passion was not. Lehigh made the prudent decision to close for the rest of the semester.

Mother's death, the war, my failing marriage. After some months, friends who were concerned by my obvious depression, urged us to go with them on an encounter weekend. Encounter groups were popular at the time, small gatherings that encouraged openness to oneself and others. Arturo wasn't interested. I left Omar with him and went alone. At first I was wary and tried to keep myself to myself, but the facilitator made me feel comfortable and encouraged me to share my feelings, something very new to me. At the sessions I wept and wept. For once I was not polite or reserved.

I returned renewed, released, full of sexual energy. For a few weeks I tempted and cajoled Arturo to sex. That ended when I learned I was pregnant. I tried to convince myself Arturo was worried he would injure the baby, but I knew that wasn't the problem.

When Sara was born I was once again passionately in love with a baby.

Sara

You are such an easy baby,
sleep through the night,
nurse three times a day.
I am charmed by your milky
snuffles and grunts,
the clutch of your fist
around my finger.

In the little sunroom,
windows all around,
I rock you in my arms,
feel the speedy beat
of your heart
while sheer white curtains
stir in summer wind.

For those days
we are content,
dreaming in a world
of blue toile, filmy light.

Pleasure derived from Sara and Omar. After Sara was born, Arturo did not touch me again.

I did not complete my thesis for my m.a. I stayed home with the children and took part-time jobs I could do at home.

In 1975, when Sara was five and Omar ten, the three of us went home to Vermont to be with my father as he died from stomach cancer.

The Stone

This stone in my hand
is oblong with white streaks,
a marbling of fat in meat,
lamb perhaps, because one side
is rough, opaque as the fell
left on the lamb after the wool
is stripped away.

The color is not the color of meat
but of milk and butterscotch,
or of the graham crackers drizzled
with honey and milk my father
ate at night in the kitchen in Vermont
sitting alone at the white table,
or of the apricot jam he bought
in Beirut by the five pound jar
to spread on fine-textured French bread.

The texture of the stone
is like nothing living—hard, cool,
clear to the depths on two sides,
reassuring, something to roll in the hand,
like one from the string of worry beads
he bought and carried behind him,
he, a tall Swede with hairy knuckles
and strong hands, turning the smooth stones
as he walked daily through the *souks*,
a beret over his fine straight hair. His eyes,
behind receding spirals of gold-rimmed glasses,
above his incurving beak of a nose,
full of questions and delight.

Beirut was still the Paris of the Middle East
then, a zesty stewpot of lamb and thyme
simmering on cedar logs brought down
from the mountains. It was still years
until my father's stomach sealed itself
and he starved without complaint
in a quiet bedroom only able to cast out
strings of yellow mucus into the white
enamel pot brought down from the attic.

His beautiful massive bones, elegant
against the white sheets, gradually
superseding the daily starbursts
of blue and purple veins, the yellow flesh
superfluous, shining, hard.

Arturo and I were divorced a year after my father's death. I had
expected marriage to be for me what it had been for my mother. She
could depend on my father to take charge when she needed him. I had
seen my father's surreptitious pats and pinches to Mother's bottom
when he thought we weren't looking, the kisses they exchanged when
he left the house and then again when he returned, how much they
valued each other's opinions. I wanted to be desired and cherished as
she had been.

Mother, in a conversation before my wedding, observed that
many girls married men who resembled their fathers. Arturo didn't
seem to be anything at all like my father. At the time I didn't pay much
attention. I thought Arturo's exoticism was simply an interesting
addition. And I never considered the other, more fundamental
problem.

Still, I'm not sure I would have had the courage to divorce if my
parents had lived. Whatever reservations they had about Arturo,
they did not believe in divorce. I would have been afraid to face their
imagined disappointment and disapproval.

Because of Granddaddy Nuquist's business acumen and my
parents' frugality, I was cushioned by an inheritance sufficiently large
to make the break. I knew I could get by for at least a year. I did and
I have.

A Last Word from Mother

Considering all your advantages
you've done less with them than
I hoped.

Perhaps people who can't do, write.
I used to call you Harum Scarum.
How right I was!

The time you waste hunting misplaced
books, files, e-mails—you were
always easily distracted, pell-mell
into topsy-turvy.

Order did not come naturally to me
either , but I was able to discipline
myself.

Oh, but you were good company.
My, didn't we talk. Together we
worried over the issues of the day.
Those were bad times, too—the struggle
for civil rights, the assassinations, the war
in Vietnam, the changing roles of women—
always something to discuss.

As your father grew more conservative
with age, you and I became allies to the left,
at least in thought.

I see that despite, or perhaps
because of, your easygoing nature,
you've managed to have an interesting life.
Of course, you've lived, as they say,
in interesting times.

(By the way, I wouldn't have been
happy, but I would have
understood your divorce. I loved you,
you know.)

Waking the Woman in the Attic

I had thought to kill her.
I assumed she would die
if I left her there
without food and water,
and that, after a while,
I wouldn't remember
her anymore.

One day after all those years
she was tapping on the attic floor again.
I didn't have the energy not to think
about her, so I decided to let her out.

She's been down here
a long time now.
Not at all what I expected — so ordinary —
she too is afraid of the telephone
and she eats far too much. She wastes hours
pretending. Full of these embarrassing longings
(that she's evidently willing to tell to anybody),
she's all yearning, all need. From time to time
she escapes into my poems.

Afterword

Dear Andy,

This morning when I ate my yoghurt,
unsweetened, runny, I thought of the culture,
dried on a clean cotton handkerchief, our father
brought home from Lebanon, fifty-four years ago.
As long as he lived he kept it alive, a fresh
batch every week or so in the stainless pot you use
now to continue his tradition.
Its sharp flavor, smooth texture, often
relegated to the back of the refrigerator, but never
abandoned. You have always been a man of ritual
and discipline.
Now this is the last living link to any
generation before the one you and I share.
It comforts me. Your sister, Elizabeth

Author's Note

In the early 1990s I spent time researching my Quaker roots in the records collected and stored at the Friends Historical Library of Swarthmore College in Pennsylvania. In 1992 I packed my jeep with file folders of materials I had gathered and questions I hoped to answer and traveled westward from my home in Pennsylvania as my ancestors had done before me. I wanted to verify stories I had been told and to match them with the information I had gathered in the Quaker archives. During my six weeks on the road I stopped at county courthouses; newspaper offices; and college, historical society, and city libraries. With plat maps in hand I walked property lines and looked at old houses and home sites in Ohio, Illinois, Iowa, and eastern Nebraska. I read headstones in cemeteries.

My sister-in-law, Reidun Nuquist, a librarian, flew out to meet me in Lincoln, Nebraska. We spent several long days at the Nebraska Historical Society reading microfiche and examining old books and dusty files. Then the two of us drove to Beaver Valley, northwest of Valentine, Nebraska, to see where my mother's family had lived, before we continued on to a family reunion at Fort Robinson.

Of course, much of that research did not find a home in *Ransomed Voices*, but I hope what I have included enriches the book. In the intervening years I have lost the names of the many, many people who helped me in my searches, but I am grateful for their generous assistance.

Notes

Dedication page—"Silence is all we dread. / There's Ransom in a Voice—." Emily Dickinson, excerpt: J 1251 / F 1300. Reprinted by permission of the publishers and the Trustees of Amherst College from *The Poems of Emily Dickinson*, Thomas H. Johnson, ed. (Cambridge, Mass.: The Belknap Press of Harvard University Press, © 1951, 1955, 1979, 1983 by the President and Fellows of Harvard College).

p. 9—Vachel Lindsay, "The Potatoes' Dance," 56, and Irene Rutherford McLeod, "Lone Dog," 125, both from *Silver Pennies: A Collection of Modern Poems for Boys and Girl*. Blanche Jennings Thompson, ed. (New York: The Macmillan Company, 1937).

p. 10—Who is Silvia?" Song by Franz Schubert, text by William Shakespeare, from *Two Gentlemen of Verona*. "Ballad" modified version "Ballads of Herself, III" Elizabeth Raby, *The Hard Scent of Peonies* (Emmaus, Pa.: Jasper Press, 1990).

p. 15—Excerpt from letters written to Edith Nuquist, January 1941, from Elizabeth (Bessie) Wilson and Maud Nuquist, in the author's possession.

p. 17—Saint Vitus Dance—named for a third-century child martyr invoked by those who suffer from this illness, also known as Sydenham's chorea, a complication of a childhood streptococcal infection that can last for months. *The Merck Manual of Medical Information, Home Edition*, Robert Berkow, Andrew J. Fletcher, and Robert M. Bogin, eds. (Whitehouse Station, N.J.: Merck Research Laboratories, 1997), 1303.

p. 24—Advertisement in *Folkets Van* (Stromsburg, Neb.), Dec. 24, 1885, p. 2

A. Nuquist—Dealer in groceries and spices
has a complete stock of 'Groceries,' 'Provisions,' and 'Queensware.'

Deals besides in clothing, boots, and shoes.
Sells the best herring on the globe!
EGGS and BUTTER received in exchange for groceries.
My goods are genuine, the prices moderate and the service
   excellent.
Countrymen, visit me.

Translated from the Swedish by Reidun Nuquist; copy and translation in the author's possession.

pp. 24–28—Taken from the letters written by Andrew F. Nuquist to Maud Edgerton from November 1903 to June 1904; in the author's possession.

p. 29—James Arthur Edgerton, *Glimpses of the Real* (Denver: The Reed Publishing Company, 1903), 77–78. The book is a collection of editorials that originally appeared in the *Rocky Mountain News.*

p. 30—"Against Their Wishes," *Grand Island Daily Independent,* Grand Island, Neb., March 22, 1895.

pp. 32–35—From Maud Edgerton's letters to Andrew F. Nuquist, November 1903 to June 1904; in the author's possession.

pp. 36–50 Excerpts from letters written by Edith Wilson Nuquist to Andrew Edgerton Nuquist, October 1943–April, 1944, in the author's possession.

p. 55—Andrew Edgerton Nuquist taught in Lu Ho Middle School, T'unghsien, Hopei, China, 1927–1930.

p. 65—Ruth Comfort Mitchell, "The Vinegar Man," *Silver Pennies,* 108.

p. 67—"Scrape all food particles...." *This Woman* (Chicago: Virtual Artists Collective, 2012), 20.

p. 69—"Two Weeks in 1948," *The Year the Pears Bloomed Twice* (Chicago: Virtual Artists Collective, 2009), 45; also in *Ten Degrees Above Zero* (Emmaus, Pa.: Jasper Press, 2005).

p. 70—"Romance," *The Year the Pears Bloomed Twice,* 44; also in *Ten Degrees above Zero.*

pp. 82–85—"The Campaign" appeared in a slightly different form in *Vermont History* 72 (summer/fall 2004), 172–77.

p. 97—An excerpt from a letter in the author's possession from Elizabeth (Bessie) Jackson Wilson to Edith Wilson Nuquist, May 21, 1947. Granddaddy (Walter H.) Wilson was retiring from the Minneapolis Friends Meeting, his last pastorate.

Poem adapted from "The Preacher," *This Woman,* 26.

p. 107—Marion Dix Sullivan, "The Blue Juniata," 1841. Apparently, Junietta's mother mis-remembered the lyrics. The River, Juniata, became the girl, Junietta; "jetty" locks became "pretty" locks, and "many" tresses became "wavy" tresses.

pp. 106–13 and 115–18—Junietta's story comes from a transcription made by Edith Nuquist in 1968 of Junietta's untitled, unpaginated, handwritten diary in two sections: the first is an account of an

1890 excursion to Yellowstone Park written during their trip; the second is an account of experiences during Junietta and Ancie's homesteading years, 1884–1890, in Sheridan County, Neb., written about 1934 according to internal evidence. The author's great-aunt, Leone Jackson, transcribed and published the Yellowstone narrative and included it in a chapbook of her poetry, *Now & Then*, illustrated by her students at Our Lady of Rosary School, mailed out for Christmas, 1988.

pp. 113–15—Quotations and information from newspaper accounts compiled by Don Huls, ed., "The Winter of 1890 (What Happened at Wounded Knee)" (privately printed, 1988), 10, 12, 25, 33, and 73. I purchased this compilation in July 1992 at the Museum of the Fur Trade, Chadron, Neb. I also found David Humphreys Miller, *Ghost Dance* (Lincoln: University of Nebraska Press, 1985), an invaluable counterpoint, told from a Native American point of view, to Junietta's narrative of Wounded Knee and the many complicated events that preceded the tragedy.

p. 117—Ansalem and Junietta Jackson's land consisted of most of Section 34, Township 34N, Range 46W, Sheridan County.

p. 128—"Recess," *This Woman* (Chicago: Virtual Artists Collective, 2012), 24.

p. 132—Paul Gallico, *The Abandoned* (New York: Alfred A. Knopf, 1950).

p. 140—J.S. Bach, "Erbarme dich, mein Gott, *St. Matthew Passion,* sung by Marian Anderson, *Bach, Brahms, Schubert,* The RCA Victor Vocal Series, BMG Music, Inc. 1989 (originally recorded before 1972).

p. 143—James Baldwin, "Sonny's Blues," *Going to Meet the Man* (New York: Dial Press, 1965).

pp. 143–49—"The Driver" appeared under the title "The Enduring Shame of the Land of the Free," in *Welcomat* 16:36 (Philadelphia: March 25–31, 1987) in slightly different form.

p. 144—Will Thomas, *The Seeking* (New York: A.A. Wynn, Inc., 1953).

p. 171—Notice in *The Arapahoe Pioneer* 1:7 (Sept. 12, 1879):

In another column will be found the land agency card of J.W. Edgerton of this place. Parties intending purchasing land will do well to give him a call, as he is agent for the railroad lands in this vicinity, and has also a choice lot of claims, and 'prooved up' lands, placed in his hands for sale. If you have land to sell you can do no better than to place it in his hands.

The other column listed "J.W. Edgerton, Attorney-at-Law, Notary Public and Real Estate Agent. Land Laws a Specialty," both in the author's possession. See also Elizabeth Raby, "Maud E. Nuquist, First Woman Candidate for Governor of Nebraska: 'Yours for Political Housecleaning,'" *Nebraska History* 7:1 (spring 1998), 14–23.

pp. 179–80—*Time, Newsweek, Redbook, The New York Post, The Boston Sunday Globe, The New York Herald Tribune, Life Magazine,* and many other publications carried articles about Miss Blanding's speech. She herself wrote in an article for the November 1962 issue of *McCall's* (162): "I, for one, do not accept self-indulgence and moral laxity, however well rationalized, as a desirable direction of change. Man, unlike any other species, does not need to learn from experience."

p. 185—Excerpt from poem, "Legacies," *The Year the Pears Bloomed Twice,* 12. "Legacies" was also published in the journal *The Ice Man* in the 1980s.

p. 194—Martin Luther King, Jr., quoted in the column Annie's Mailbox in the Jan. 20, 2003 edition of *The Santa Fe New Mexican* in honor of Rev. King's birthday.

p. 200–01—*High Point* (N.C.) *Enterprise,* June 11 and June 12, 1963.

p. 203—Excerpt from "The Pleasures of Landscape," *The Year the Pears Bloomed Twice,* 14. The poem was also published in *The Hard Scent of Peonies.*

p. 204—"Carnivorous" in a slightly different form received an honorable mention in the Tupelo Press Poetry Project: Spring 2011 Selections.

pp. 204–5—For an excellent history of the American Field Service see AFS Norge Internasjonal Utveksling, *The AFS Story; Journeys of a Lifetime 1914*1947*1997* (Lausanne, Switz: JPM Publications S.A., 1997).

p. 221—"Mother," *The Year the Pears Bloomed Twice,* 46. The poem also appeared in *The Hard Scent of Peonies.* "Candidate," *This Woman,* 33.

p. 224—"The Stone," *The Year the Pears Bloomed Twice,* 49. The poem also appeared in *The Hard Scent of Peonies.*

p. 227—A version of "Waking the Woman in the Attic" titled "Waking Up Two Mornings in a Row" appeared in *The Year the Pears Bloomed Twice,* 17, and in *The Hard Scent of Peonies.*

Index

Page numbers in *italics* indicate photographs.
Page numbers in **boldface** indicate narrative in the person's voice.

List of Poems